Advance Praise for *A*

"Monica writes stories about food, but often they are really stories about searching. She looks for what the world will reveal if you ask questions of the things we usually keep silent. She's a generous writer, seeking the finer, richer sides of us." - *Francis Lam, Editor-at-Large, Clarkson Potter, and New York Times Magazine columnist*

"Monica Bhide is more than a food writer. She's a chronicler of culture and family history. She is a romantic for the bond between parent and child. She is an essayist of her own heart and mind, fearlessly searching for the truth in both. She is endlessly fascinating to read." - *Tim Carman, James Beard award-winning food writer for the Washington Post.*

"Monica Bhide's unbridled devotion to food, words, family, and history is crystal clear in this delicious collection. Whatever Monica's subject — her father as a young boy, the connection between her family and their mouthwatering food, or the importance of saving recipes — she writes with warmth, a keen eye, and an open and abundant heart." - *Elissa Altman, author of Poor Man's Feast*

"Monica Bhide weaves magical spells with her words. Brilliantly describing cuisines & stories that echo the chimes of a far away land while somehow simultaneously making one feel as if they are in her very backyard. Monica is magician with both words & food" *Chef Maneet Chauhan, judge on Food Nework's Chopped.*

"In her cookbook and column, Monica Bhide writes about food with knowledge and authority and love, taking the reader on a colorful and delicious tour of her native land. But cooking, she also knows, is more than just what shows up on the plate, and in this evocative and searching book she takes us deep into culture, family, history and the daily traumas and joys and wonders of a life of engagement, purpose and passion." *Todd Kliman, a James Beard Award-winning food critic for The Washingtonian*

"Fair warning: Monica Bhide's latest food essay collection will make you hungry—but not just for food, but for life. Skillfully written, with heart and soul, A Life of Spice is a rich feast for the senses." - **Mollie Cox Bryan, author of the Agatha-Award nominated** *Scrapbook of Secrets: A Cumberland Creek Mystery*

"In writing that's as mystical and real as the scent of spices heating in a pan, Monica Bhide tells the story of her connections in the kitchen in a way that everyone who loves food - whether they cook or not - can understand and adore. This book is a treat." - *Debbie Moose, author of "Southern Holidays: A Savor the South Cookbook"*

"Monica Bhide had me at Indian Onion Rings and Mangos and Champagne. Here is a woman, alive with creation, who connects at the deepest level with food and the table. My head explodes when I read a Monica Bhide story — I infer so much not just about Indian food but about the Indian psyche. What she delivers is a nuanced portrait of her sub-continental culture on a plate, with all the delicacy, passion and turmeric it deserves. *Chalo, khanna kao!*" —***Alison Singh Gee, author of Where the Peacocks Sing: A Palace, a Prince and the Search for Home***

'In these deliciously wrought essays, Monica Bhide reminds us that food is a lifeline, both real and figurative to which we all grasp. Written with transporting detail and emotional clarity, A Life of Spice, comprises themes that transcend culture or kitchen taking the reader to a delicious place where every flavor tantalizes the senses with deeper and deeper layers of understanding about ourselves and the others with whom we share our tables. Spanning India, the Middle East, and America, A Life of Spice is an essayist's journey to the most hidden recesses of the soul—and it is a journey that the reader is luckily enough to join, if only for a brief, delectable time." ***Ramin Ganeshram, author of Stir it Up and FutureChefs***

"Monica's stories take us on a journey through time, across continents and cultures. With her we fast and feast for love, we share the wonder of fairy tales with a child, we feel the longing for a lost homeland, we delight in culinary discoveries, and we find our own identity in a new land. Throughout Monica reminds us that the essence of food is love—love for our family, our history, our humanity." ***Elise Bauer, Creator of SimplyRecipes.com***

A Life of Spice

Stories of Food, Culture, and Life

Monica Bhide

Photos by Simi Jois

CONTENTS

Introduction

Dinner party conversations about my profession fascinate me. In nine out of ten instances, there will be one person who, when they find out I write about food for a living, turns to me and says, "You mean you actually like to cook? Why? I love to watch food shows on TV but who has the time to cook every day at home?" The look this person gives me is familiar: a mixture of true surprise, a little bit of astonishment, a dash of pity, and sometimes a touch of envy.

I am not ashamed to admit I love to cook. But even more than cooking, I love to eat. I am totally and completely in love with food. I traverse the spectrum from cooking really well to really poorly, but regardless of how the final dish turns out, the food I cook is my solace.

As a child, I found that experimenting in the kitchen gave me a deep satisfaction, even as I would cook up disasters: breads hard as rocks; mousse frozen solid; tomatoes floating, bloated, in lentil soups; and more. When I made ghee (clarified butter) for the first time, I burnt the pan and the butter. When I made it for the second time, I burnt more butter. The third time, my mother prayed to the heavens that I would stop. At age ten I gutted a fish and then cried for a week for forgiveness: the scales hung around nooks and crannies in the kitchen for what seemed like a year. I have been trying to learn how to cut up a whole chicken since I was eighteen. (On the plus side, I believe in reincarnation, so I have several lives left to learn how to do it right.) The more I cooked, the more curious I became as to what made something taste good versus bad.

My oldest son, who loves to be in the kitchen, remarked once that his favorite sound in the house (other than football on TV) was the sound of frying *papads*—lentil wafers that I fry with feverish obsession—a few times a week. I urged him on, and he added that the sweet smell of the cardamom oatmeal I make for him lures him out of bed each morning.

I grew up in a cozy, delicately furnished apartment in the heart of the Middle Eastern island of Bahrain, a tiny dot in the Arabian Gulf. Before bed, I would wander into the small, efficient kitchen to see what was soaking, drying, being pickled, or laid out for the meal the next day. A bowl of lentils soaked in water would enlist a groan, whereas a countertop filled with onions and garlic and tomatoes (for chopping the next morning) would mean a yummy curry would be on the table. Yogurt inside a cheesecloth and hanging from the kitchen faucet, cans set atop homemade cheese to dry it out, random vegetables placed in various baskets or brown paper bags to ripen, a token food—like a can of baked beans—from Dad's travel around the world ... all filled my childhood days.

My love of eating made me very nosy about entering other people's kitchens. As I watched them cook, I asked questions. One aunt's bangles jingled merrily as she explained the difference between making a real *masala* versus the "fake, fast, and useless" masalas her servants made. Another aunt's eyes gleamed as she told me about all the bread and butter I ate as a toddler. I asked questions and they answered. Then they would hand me the knife and show me how to chop things just right. Finally, they delivered what is to me the sign of ultimate respect: they allowed me to season their dishes—to add the spices in the right order and in the right combination.

It wasn't just aunts and uncles and other family members who instilled in me this love of cooking. In our Delhi home we had servants who had mastered the art of making meals. From them I would learn what *not* to do with a pressure cooker, how to make the right combination of spices so that one did not dominate the others. It was a job for them, yet when I asked them questions, their eyes would light up and pleasure would return to their faces. That look said, "I matter."

As I grew older and cooked more, I discovered that food connected me to people in ways that little else did. In coaxing recipes from people, I would often get stories of their loves and losses, their secrets, and their dreams. The food was often only a symbol of something else. I spent days learning to make a dish that I already knew, just so I could be close to my friend who was teaching me. I began to pretend to hate avocadoes, for they reminded me of the time my friend, while teaching me how to make guacamole, began to cry as she revealed she had cancer. Another friend just refused to cook for her children because of fear they would reject her because she was a terrible cook. One shared a potato dish her mother taught her. It was the only dish that she remembered from her childhood—her mother had died when she was very young.

I began to learn how to listen to people as they talked and taught me about food. The stories behind a broken knife, the love of an old spatula, the reason for making a sauce a particular way, all seem to have one thing in common: memories. And all the memories had one thing in common: they define who we are today.

Not all my friends cook. Some refuse to step into the kitchen. Some can barely boil water. But they all have stories to tell about eating in amazing, off-the-beaten-path places. I have friends who take on amazing food adventures; I have cousins who can tell me which stall in Old Delhi makes the best *paranthas*—a type of Indian griddle bread. A friend in Washington, D.C., showed me a grocery store nearby in Virginia that sells the most delightful Indian street food. Another friend in Mumbai invites me over and orders delightful takeout from places I never heard of. They all share a common bond: the love of food. Their memories of food are funny, haunting, inspiring, connecting. A meal shared with them means one thing: I now have a part of them that will connect me with them forever. I shared a memory.

Sometimes, a memory is all you have. I lost a friend several years ago, but the meals shared with her, the laughter as she failed to understand my lack of appreciation for beer, my wonderment at her inability to eat anything spiced with more than just salt, our shared love of pierogis. It is all there, stored in my mind for the days when I am offered pale ale or find pierogis in the freezer section of the grocery store.

Another close friend died very young, at twenty-five. I remember him as a child, his mother chasing him around the table, begging him to eat one bite of his dinner. When I complain about my kids not eating and need to hunt them down for dinner, that memory comes back: haunting, painful, real, and sobering. It reminds me to count my blessings, each day. My parents are far away from me and I have memories of cooking for them that keep me warm: I revel in the fact that my lamb curry could get my father to clap and say, "This is simply amazing, child," and then he would offer me more time in the kitchen to grow my beginner skills.

Oddly for someone who adores food and cooking, I once wrote a story about why, as an adult, I don't cook for my parents. It incited hate mail. People were upset that I "don't take care of my aging parents" as they perceived it. But they missed the point. I am always in the kitchen with my parents when they cook. I cut, I chop, I wash, I clean—but I won't go to the stove. That is where the magic happens; that is where my parents perform their rituals that I grew to love. They season, they stir, they sauté, and I stand back in reverence. I eat, and I clean. I walk away filled with gratitude. The new memories are there now, tucked away for the next time I wake up missing my mother's chickpeas.

Food memories have nurtured me in difficult times and I find myself constantly drawn to the kitchen. Sometimes I am in there for hours and don't cook a thing. I pick a spice and dream about it. I wonder what cumin could do to a pork chop. I smell the aromas from my cabinet and am transported to a time in Agra when I fell in love with the taste of creamy lentils, to a time in Bahrain when the smell of cumin-scented chicken sizzling on a hot grill brought my nose to attention, to a quiet morning spent sipping cardamom tea with my mother, to cooking an oregano-laced pizza for my boys.

The spirit of my kitchen seems to dictate my actions for the day. Each morning, I wake up to a cup of steaming coffee prepared by my husband of eighteen years. The kitchen, every day, has a different energy. Some mornings, I feel it invites me to be a part of its magic, enticing me to pick up a knife, to smell the fresh lemons on the counter, or bite into the juicy grapes in the bowl. There are other days when it seems like the energy is quieter, as though I am invited to stay, but not mess with the hearth or the heart of the kitchen. I order takeout on those days. It was years before I realized that the spirit of my kitchen was a reflection of the energy that I brought into it each day. My kitchen walls hold stories of heartbreak that friends revealed over cups of steaming tea; they bear the scars of a husband and wife disagreeing over life decisions; they bear witness to two young boys growing up to be men of taste and talent. We spend our lives in the kitchen, regardless of the fact that there may or may not be any active cooking going on at the time.

Traveling the world and discovering new ingredients have strengthened my love affair with cooking and turned it into an obsession. I love to eat new things, to find new tastes, to incorporate them into my own creations. Sometimes, I succeed:

I can do amazing things with *sambal*—a spicy sauce used in many Asian cuisines like Malaysian—and contend that in a previous life I was probably Malay. And there are disasters: there is no place in coffee for sriracha (don't ask).

I don't expect people to love food as I do. It is not something that can be taught. A passion for food comes from within. To me, food is about people and creating memories. Cooking nurtures my spirit, and the food I cook allows me the blessing of nurturing those around me.

***

A Life of Spice is about my torrid romance with food. Just as with any romance, there have been moments of great heartache, unbelievable happiness, betrayals, breakups, and of course, intimacy. The essays in this book showcase how food affects all the areas of our lives: family, friends, children, love, culture, faith, and more. *A Life of Spice* captures the delights of cooking as wooing and food as nurturer, as well as the sadness of the heartbreak kitchen.

Just one more thing: To be true to the title of the book, I have sprinkled some of my favorite spices along the way. I hope you enjoy!

How It All Began

Author's Note: Before I share my food essays with you, I feel compelled to share this story. This is how it all began for my family. I felt it critical to try and understand where we came from. Understanding the past provides a great foundation on which we build our future.

This story is excerpted from my upcoming food memoir. I have taken some editorial license here with the details and some of the names have been changed to protect the privacy of those featured here.

The Traveling Bread

Intricate patterns of fish and peacocks are etched deeply into the fine wooden dining table, providing perfect hiding places for tiny marble dice. The little boy knows the crevices in the table, carved by a local craftsman who also created the elaborate mirror frames on the wall, will be beyond the reach of his younger brother.

"Go, *beta*, call everyone. Dinner is ready," announces his mother as he hurries to hide the last die. He looks up at her and grimaces. She usually calls him by his first name and only says *beta*—son—when he does something wrong. The sprawling bungalow overflows with relatives from around the city. Stained glass windows are thrown open wide to allow cool air into the vast room. A servant rhythmically pulls a thick rope that waves a muslin cloth canopy attached high above, near the ceiling, sucking the heat upward and providing a refreshing breeze of circulated air. Dust storms haven't arrived yet but the sky is threatening. Oversized paintings of Sufi saints, silken sheets with poetry, and deep maroon Persian rugs line the walls.

The *beta* mention is quickly forgotten as the little boy comes out from under the dinner table to see what is being placed on it. "Mummy, you've made meat curry," he says and claps his hands enthusiastically as he points to the aromatic curry garnished with small fried potatoes. The dinner table, draped with a silk blue tablecloth, overflows with an abundance of family favorites. Beside the curry is a grand bowl of turmeric-scented rice studded with fresh green peas, a terra-cotta pot of gleaming white yogurt, a brass platter of thinly sliced fried okra "ladies fingers" with toasted cumin, and a bowl of baby onions bathed in lemon juice. A water-filled terra-cotta pitcher, the young boy's favorite utensil, rests quietly on a side table. He loves that it somehow magically chills the water on hot summer days like today.

His mother's characteristic blue bowl painted with elaborate white and orange flowers in *kashi* style by local potters, overflowing with white jasmine from their garden, sits majestically in the middle of the table. The flowers' gentle sweet scent is no match for the wafting aroma of cumin and cinnamon.

"Yes, I made it just as *nani*, your grandma, makes it. The way you love it—with the fried potatoes," says the boy's mother, waving her bangle-laden arms in the air. "Now go call everyone before the *phulkas* (tasty griddle breads) come out." She turns instinctively to instruct a beloved family servant, Das. "Be sure to bring out the fresh ghee—clarified butter—with the *phulkas* today. The one last week seemed a bit off." The old servant nods and rushes into the busy kitchen.

12

The often-boisterous family, comprised of numerous generations and degrees of cousins, usually arrives at the table famished. But today, the young boy notices, the adults are dragging: there are whispers and stolen glances. *Something is wrong,* he senses, as even the cinnamon-scented curry cannot distract them.

His mother, blessed with graceful waist-length flowing black hair, gentle features, enchanting eyes, and natural beauty— lovingly called Hawa or "Eve"—begins dinner by serving a savory, lemony lotus stem *chaat*—a family-favorite snack—to the quiet group. Pointing to a small woven basket at the far end of the dining room, filled with white jasmine and yellow marigolds, Hawa says to the other women at the table, "The monsoon came so late this year, but you know I was at the Chenab River this morning and it is overflowing. Everything is in bloom."

There are attempts at smiles. In truth, Hawa came in crying from her visit to the river that morning. In addition to the flowers blooming, there was something she had not seen before: bodies. She pleaded with her husband, "Don't say anything in front of the children. My city of saints, Multan, is dying a terrible death. There seems to be no scent in the jasmine I picked … a sign of respect for the dead."

Multan, her city of birth, is built on a high mound of the ruins of ancient cities. It gets its name, the story goes, from the Sanskrit word *Mul* or beginning. Among its many rulers was Alexander the Great. The city survived rule by the Moghuls, the Chinese, the Sikhs, but now this birthplace of the oldest Hindu religious text, the Rig Veda, home to the Sun God's Temple of the Sun, is being cut out from its mother India and handed over to the newly created Muslim Pakistan.

At the table, there isn't a place for everyone, so the little children crowd into a circle on a small woven brown and black Persian rug. "Why isn't anyone eating?" the little boy tugs at Hawa's shirt. "Usually when the *phulkas* come out piping hot, everyone fights over them."

Hawa brings a finger up to her lips and signals the boy to be quiet. He rips a bit of *phulka* and dips it gingerly into the robust curry. He picks up a meat bone and tries to suck the tasty marrow out, just as he has seen his father do countless times, but it refuses to budge.

He walks over to his father for help, but quietly backs away when his grand-uncle Choudhry Sidhu, a short, stout man with a loud voice, stands to speak.

"I have been the Municipal Commissioner for Multan and I can tell you they will never be able to partition our India. Never." His normally steady voice quivers with anger and righteousness.

"It is your position, the fact that everyone knows you: this is what will make us a target of the rioters. The partition is already happening," says Choudhry Govind angrily. The boy has never heard his father speak in that angry tone before.

Sidhu retorts, "I went to jail to keep this country together, not to rip it apart."

"There is rioting everywhere. Even our walled city is not safe anymore! We have to face the reality: India is now divided, and our beloved Multan is no more part of the new India," Aunty Satto interjects as she adjusts her thick-rimmed glasses on her

narrow nose. "We have children; we must think of something."
She almost never speaks up; the little boy is now intrigued.

Hawa is busy serving more food onto everyone's plate,
hoping a bite or two will settle disturbed spirits and angry voices.

"It is a sin to waste food; we must eat." There are a few
minutes of quiet at Hawa's insistence. "What if this is our last
…" Her voice trails off as she hides her face and her tears in her
red silk *duppata*.

Some begin to eat their rice and curry, others just stare at
their plate.

"You saw what happened two days ago?" shouts Choudhry
Sidhu, now towering over the table, his hands pounding angrily
on the wood. "When the women were in danger, our Muslim
brothers accompanied their caravan here, to our home, to safety.
They are our family." His voice echoes large in the dining room
even as he struggled to fight back his tears. "We are still one
country of brothers."

"I agree," said Hawa. "As has always been said: *Saain Raaje
Badal Wendan, par Prajaa Kadian Nahin Badaldi:* A country
may change its rulers, but the people never lose their country."

One of the cousins picks up a small onion and crushes it
between his hands. He then peels it and offers it to the young
boy. "Thank you, *bhaiya*, brother," says the boy.

Usually, all the men would do this. But today no one is
interested in onions, *phulkas*, or meat curry.

The servant, Das, has now placed a sweet roti in front of the
children to distract them from all the tension at the main table.
The bread's gooey, sugary texture with the smell of cardamom
is too much for the little boy to resist.

"What shall I buy from the market tomorrow?" Das asks Hawa, as is customary at the end of dinner. She looks at him with tears in her kohl-rimmed black eyes and shakes her head gently. *Nothing*.

"Das, there is no *sohan halwa* today?" the little boy inquires. Usually with so many people in the house, *sohan halwa*, a dish made with ghee, nuts, milk, sugar, and flour, is almost always on the table. His mother often regales him with magnificent tales of how hundreds of years ago, Mughal Emperor Humayun came to India from Persia and bought the halwa with him.

"No, *beta*, I could not make it today," says Das, lying as kindly as he can. "But I will make it for you tomorrow." His answer appeases the little boy.

Choudhry Govind returns to the room. His dark skin is flushed, and he is wiping away his sweat—maybe tears—with a small, starched white handkerchief. No one had noticed that he had gotten up and left a while ago to take a call.

"I just got off the phone with Aunty Lajjo."

"Yes, yes, Lajjo is in Delhi now, right?" Aunty Satto asks.

"She says the conditions are getting worse. She is insistent that if we want to stay alive, we need to leave Multan. There are reports of buses ...trains ... filled with dead bodies going across the border ... both ways." The boy's father Govind can barely utter the words as their meaning starts to sink in.

"What? I don't want to leave Multan," the little boy protests, but his voice is drowned out in the chaos as women begin to cry and the men's voices get louder in protest.

On hearing the commotion, the servants rush out of the kitchen into the dining room.

"Trilok will arrive before dawn from Delhi, and he will fly us out. He and Lajjo say it is our only chance to leave ... alive," says his father and then glances around the room. "There is more."

"The Muslim workers from our factory are outside now. They will do what they can to protect us though this night. They tell me that they have seen the rioters heading toward our mills. There isn't much time left. It could be a matter of hours before the rioters come here ... hours or, or sooner ..."

As the eldest member of the family, Choudhry Sidhu stands up and turns to the family. He looks straight ahead and at no one in particular. In his most imposing voice, he announces, "We leave tomorrow before the sun lights up the fields."

The decision is made and everyone begins to get up and look at each other. No one seems to know what to do. How do you pack up a lifetime?

"There is no time to worry now," says Choudhry Sidhu looking at his confused and anxious family. "Take only the best clothes you can wear, your money and jewelry. We will come back for the rest. Now go!"

"We will need food," Hawa says.

"I can make *doli ki roti*, and I can pack *achar* pickles," Das offers. *Doli ki roti* is traditional travel fare, a dish of whole wheat bread leavened using spices and stuffed with lentils and dry fruits. It is prepared in an earthen pot called *doli*, and a romantic tale says that because it is given to a bride on her long journey to her new home, this bread doesn't need preservatives.

"Das, that takes days to prepare, and at best we have a few hours," says Hawa. They disappear into the kitchen together.

The little boy stands, now alone in the large room, staring at the untouched food on the table. He rushes to his room and brings out his muslin handkerchief. He lays it out on the table, picks up the small pieces of untouched sweet roti and places them on the small cloth.

"Mummy, don't worry. I am getting the food," he calls after his mother.

Neighborhood men, dressed in starched white collarless shirts, stream in and out of the house throughout the night, each talking with Sidhu. Most are asking for his help. As the crowd dwindles, Sidhu is in deep conversation with his always swanky brother, Girdharilal. "The temple … the idol …" are the only words heard by those in the room as the two whisper to each other. Girdharilal calls for Das soon after and then the two disappear into the dark night outside.

Sidhu looks around at his quiet house, and his gaze stops at the window. It is dark outside, but it feels darker on the inside. He switches on a camel-hide lamp with glorious red and pink flowers painted on the shade. It emits a soft glow in the center of the room. He smiles as he looks at the lamp. The local *naqqashi* craftsmen outdid themselves: this is beautiful work. He sits down, perhaps for the last time, on his favorite chair, places his face in his hands and just weeps.

As the dawn arrives, the sun, Surya, blazes, pounding punishing rays on those who seek a mirage of safety. The air god, Vayu, is angry because the air is thick with smoke and the smell of charred human flesh. He refuses to provide any relief.

The airfield holds telltale signs of massacre as bloody footprints crisscross each path. But there is an eerie calm. Even the leaves aren't rustling. They are quiet, as though paying their last respects to those who are being sacrificed.

"It is time to go," his mother says gently, as she pulls the little boy off the buggy. Her hair, braided with a black threaded tassel, has tiny colorful beads that tinkle as she moves. She flows with the grace of a dancer but the firmness of a lioness protecting her cubs. She has lost one to illness already and is adamant about protecting the remaining three.

The little boy clings fiercely to his mother's bright orange *kurta* shirt, trying to hide in its promise of sanctuary.

"Where are we going, mummy?" he whispers as he struggles to undo the buttons of the dressy black long coat—a *sherwani*—his mother has dressed him in. "I don't want to go in this. I don't want to leave. I want to go home."

"We have to go, *beta*. It is not safe here anymore."

Not safe? This is the home of saints, of poets, of kings. "The people are kind here, they always call me *Hawa da putar*, the son of Hawa, when I go to the markets and are always helpful," he says, pleading to stay. His mother hugs him. "It is not the people," she said. "The people are kind and loving. It is the politicians. They are bent on dividing and destroying our country. We are lucky to be here, *beta*, we are. We are blessed that we can go. Now come." Yet Hawa knows that today they will lose everything. The whole family gathers, dressed in their cleanest clothes—a stark contrast to the bloodied tarmac. There are whispers in the crowd: "I hear brothers are killing brothers with daggers. Flames are consuming homes and children …"

Choudhry Sidhu suddenly yells, "I hear it; it is there; look up." He points to the sky as a gleaming silver DC-3 banks on its approach to land. As the aircraft pulls to a stop in front of them, others rush from the town toward the plane, hoping for an escape.

The door swings open, and the pilot appears shouting: "Move, move, we have little time," as he has witnessed fires and riots on his approach to land.

All the men, dressed in starched white *salwars* and loose fitting *kameez*, spread like milk spilling onto a table as they rush to envelope the plane. As they reach the plane, the men wearing red turbans—a sign of honor—step aside and hold back the crowd to ensure the women and children board first.

The little boy instantly recognizes the pilot in the doorway. It is his grand-uncle Trilok. The boy calls out to him but is drowned out by the roar of the crowd.

Trilok is shouting. "Get aboard quickly. But you cannot bring in anything but the clothes you have on and any money you have. No shoes, no sandals, no bags."

The young boy watches in disbelief as his mother takes off her favorite, tiny sandals—a gift embossed with a silver mesh and red velvet interior—and throws them onto the tarmac atop a growing mound of now discarded shoes—*juttis*. The *juttis*, with their intricate gold and cream embroideries, their leather bodies and their glittering *sitaras* stars, prove a stark contrast against the crumbling, dark brown ground. The boy does the same with his bright blue *juttis*. The weight of the pile equals place for one more passenger. More piles form—clothes, food tiffins, photographs—the memories of a lifetime.

"Choudhry Sahib, Choudhry Sahib," a shrill voice calls out.

From the doorway of the DC-3, Choudhry Govind sees their

loyal servant, Das, running mightily toward the aircraft. "Choudhry Sahib, the house is burning, the house is burning— we saved some things before they came. I am taking my family and we are going to the train station … thank you for everything … for the money … I pray we will see you again. We have the idol … We have it … We will bring it … We have it …"

The little boy's father is pulled into the aircraft and the door shuts.

The twenty-two seat plane is filled to the brim with multiple, shoeless passengers in every seat. Other than the pilot, no one on board has been in a plane before.

The plane, headed to now-independent, secular India, carries just a few of the refugees. In the end, more than twelve million people would be displaced, and more than four hundred thousand would lose their lives. This would be the largest human migration, more like forced expulsion, in history.

Aboard the DC-3, the young boy tugs his mother's shirt. "I am so sorry," he tells his mother. "Everyone will go hungry. I forgot the food. I made a small pouch for the rotis but I could not fit enough. I had to leave it all behind."

Hawa pulls her son in close, tucking him under her arm and resting her head on his. "I did not bring the tiffins. I left them in the *tonga*. It is not just you who could not bring the food."

A young woman shrieks out as if in pain and begins to weep. The men around her are too stunned to react to the news. "What is it? What is it?" voices shout. A headcount reveals that, in the chaos, someone has been left behind. The woman's son— only five—is not aboard the plane.

"We will come back. Don't worry," Choudhry Sidhu

proclaimed loudly. "We *will* come back for him and for our home."

The plane lands in Delhi a short while later. The stunned passengers silently spill onto the black tarmac, under a searing sun, without shoes or belongings. Without a home.

The small boy, holding his mother's hand, looks up. "Mummy, my feet are burning."

That young boy was my father.

This is the beginning of our story. A story about finding yourself and your destiny when you have lost the very thing that defines you most: your homeland.

Food and Culture

Finger Food

The disdain on my guest's face radiated such strong contempt that it could have made the yogurt on the dining room table curdle. Her arms were folded across her chest, her head tilted to one side and her eyes scrutinized my every move.

"You still eat with your hands?" she asked with much scorn as she watched me take a small piece of Indian griddle bread, dip it into a luscious red lentil curry, and place it gently in my mouth.

Before I could answer, the tirade began. The speaker, a young woman, was a friend. I would have forgiven the lecture about cleanliness, lack of culture, lack of table etiquette, and my total disregard for eating "that way" in front of my children, if she had not also been of Indian origin. While I don't expect people from other cultures to comprehend why we do things a certain way, to have someone from your own ethnicity show such ignorance made my fingers crunch up into a fist.

Food is such an intimate experience, even more so than sex.

Everything we put in our mouth touches our insides, affects how we grow, affects how we age, affects how we behave. It defines who we are. And yet there is such an aversion in many Western cultures to touching it.

When I was a child, my family and almost all our friends ate with our fingers. And we cooked with our hands, by *andaza*—estimation. My mother would dip her clean, cupped fingers into the lentil or rice jar and pick one *moothi* (handful) of the ingredient per person before adding it to her pot. The spices were measured in *jutkis* (pinches) with her fingers before adding to the pot. We had no measuring cups, no teaspoons or tablespoons, and definitely no weighing scales. And no, not because we were poor. The eggplant was held up in the palm to check its weight; we touched the mango to the nose to smell for freshness.

Once the vegetables and lentils were cooked, my mother would get into kneading the dough for the bread. Her fingers deftly worked the flour to release its magic and bind it into a mystical pile that would later, when kissed by fire, produce bread worth killing for. My grandmother would take the bread off the fire, still scorching hot, and crush it between the palms of her hands before serving it to the children. She said it softened the bread; I thought it added love.

The point of this is not whether the measures were right; they were. The point is that the food was constantly in human contact. Mint and cilantro leaves, when crushed on a granite *sil batta* (like a large mortar and pestle), have a different consistency and taste than when they are ground in a food processor. Even to this day, many cooks will tell you that using electrical appliances changes the way food tastes. It is similar to the way some ancient cultures believe that if someone takes a photo of you, he or she takes away a piece of your spirit.

Don't get me wrong—I use electrical appliances—but there is a widely held belief in India that good food is the result of "good hands." The energy of the hands is transferred to the foods that are being prepared. Two perfectly capable cooks can use the same ingredients to prepare the same dishes and yet, one's dishes may taste better than the other's. You may think it is because of cooking technique. I beg to differ. Food prepared with the energy of love tastes better.

In ancient India, it was also believed that touching food with your fingers and then putting it in your mouth brought forth the right digestive fluids to help you. Eating with your hands makes you aware of what is going in your mouth. It makes eating less of a mindless chore and more of an experience where your presence is required. I have no evidence to prove my next statement, but I stand behind it 100 percent: food eaten with your hands tastes better.

I have taught my kids to eat with their hands. And I am proud of that. Yes, when we eat out, they can use forks and knives and chopsticks better than I can. But at home, we eat as we desire, with love and abandon and with clean, washed hands.

My friend's tirade came to an end: "Are you listening? Have you heard a word I have said?"

I looked up at her. The Indian inside me wanted to scream; the hostess inside me needed to be polite. "Eating Indian food with a fork and knife, I have read," I said as graciously as I could, "is like trying to make love through an interpreter."

Despite herself she laughed, and then picked up her fork and knife. The rest of us ate with our hands. In the end, I licked my fingers for good measure.

First published in Eating Well.

A Question of Taste

It started out as a perfectly normal workday. A food writer by night, I was working at a consulting firm, in a lonely cubicle on the seventh floor of a suburban Washington, D.C. office. I worked alone, since most of my teammates were all over the United States—part of what is called a "virtual team." It sounds glamorous, but it translates into being very lonely at work. So imagine my surprise when the receptionist called me to say I had a visitor. I could hear her giggling on the other end of the phone. "Who is it?" I demanded to know. "Well," she hesitated, "it's a gentleman in a chef's uniform, and he has a picture of you holding your cookbook. Says it's from *The Washington Post*."

A chef here in my office? With my picture in hand, no less? If you live long enough you see everything, my grandmother used to say, and sure enough here it was—a chef asking for a novice writer at an HR consulting firm.

And there he was, a young man in uniform, chef's hat and

all. He extended his hand toward me, saying, "Hi, I am Jonathan Krinn, and I have just opened a new restaurant downstairs in this building. It's called 2941. My mother saw the article about you in the newspaper and told me to check you out. She thought we might enjoy meeting each other."

Those were his exact words. I thought his mother was matchmaking. It must have shown on my face. "Since you write books and I cook," he quickly added.

I wasn't sure how to react. He invited me to his kitchen to learn more about him and his cooking. And I agreed, reluctantly, not knowing what would be expected of me.

We set a date, and he left.

I took the day of our meeting off from work and arrived armed with nothing more than anxiety, for now I had Googled him and knew who he was. What on earth would we talk about, I wondered.

The interior of the restaurant looked like a new bride: perfectly adorned, a bit coy and yet very inviting. He met me at the door and led me into the kitchen. It was huge, almost as big as the restaurant. I was in awe of all the gadgets. As we chatted, a chemistry began to develop. His passion was French-American food and mine was Indian—so vastly different, and yet the soul behind them was the same.

He muttered something about showing me how to make a perfect sauce. I was completely ill at ease—my knowledge of French stopped at "*oui*"—and he was talking a mile a minute about ingredients and techniques. We were standing over the pot. And then it happened—that bewildering incident.

He took a spoon, dipped it in the sauce and then proceeded

to … dare I say, *lick it*. I was stunned. Completely horrified and stunned. He offered me some and I shook my head. "Are you okay?" he inquired.

I stuttered, "You tasted the sauce…. How could you do that? Don't you know you are not allowed to taste while you cook?"

Now it was his turn to look stunned. "I have never heard of that," he said. "How would you know when to season?"

When you least expect it, culture shows up. I had learned to cook by sight, smell, sound, and texture. In our kitchen, we were not allowed to taste. My father would teach me to roast spices and to learn that coriander whimpers, cumin smolders, mustard sizzles, and cinnamon roars. I learned to cook by sight as the colors of the spices turned, and then by smell—sweet, earthy, heady, sharp if they are roasting correctly, or unforgiving acrid smells if they burn.

My mother taught me to make curries by hearing how onions sing in oil, from a slight sizzle to a glorious harmony as they become perfectly caramelized. I learned to watch the tomatoes marry the onions. The sign the union was complete and ready for spices to be added was when the oil separated from the mixture. Roast, sizzle, temper, broil, boil, bake, simmer, sauté, fry—we had to do it all by watching and listening.

The reason, I was told many years later, was that in our house the first offering of the food was for the gods. If you tasted while you cooked, it made the food impure. My grandmother would carefully take the first piece of bread she cooked each night, place it on a plate along with a helping of all the other vegetables and lentils, and set it aside before the meal for the family was served. After we all ate, she would go outside and set the plate in front of the cows that used to hang around our neighborhood. Cows are considered sacred in the Hindu religion and feeding them is said to be akin to feeding God.

Jonathan listened carefully to my story and nodded. Then he held the spoon to me and said, "Here, taste it. There are no cows in DC."

This essay first appeared in The Washington Post.

Why We Are Afraid to Cook

My older son had just come back from school, the younger one was playing with ice cubes on the deck, and I decided in my infinite wisdom to make pad thai at home for the first time. Noodles with shrimp and sauce—how hard can that be, I thought.

First, I laid out all the ingredients I thought I would need. I asked friends for recipes and then decided I would recreate this dish based on my own tastes. (Translation: no cookbook author or recipe was harmed as a result of my effort.)

I soaked the flat, pale noodles in hot water, according to the package directions. I sliced scallions, rinsed and dried bean sprouts, whisked eggs, rinsed and pat-dried shrimp, and finely minced cilantro. I coarsely ground some peanuts and arranged the ingredients for the sauce neatly on the counter—fish sauce, tamarind paste, chili oil, and palm sugar.

I heated my wok till it was searing hot, added the eggs, scrambled, and moved them gently to the side as I added the shrimp and tossed to cook them to perfection. Next came scallions and beans sprouts, a good toss, and then the sauces and sugar went in. As a childhood habit, I never taste when I cook. It comes from the belief I was taught as a child that the first taste of prepared food is always an offering to the Gods and tasting it defiles it. When I was growing up, we would feed the first serving to neighborhood animals, since they are said to be pure of soul. Here in the U.S., I say a prayer before serving the food.

Now, back to the pad thai. I had already rinsed the noodles in cold water and they went in next. My first attempt at the pad thai was ready. I was concerned that the color did not quite resemble restaurant pad thai, but let it go. In fact, it looked like a sad brown instead of a vibrant orange. But undeterred, I went on.

I shouldn't have.

The dish tasted abysmal. No, the noodles weren't mushy, the shrimp weren't overcooked, the eggs did not get rubbery. None of that. The dish had no taste. We would have been better off eating toast without butter. Even that would have tasted better. My children, bless their heart, poured ketchup on it in an attempt to eat it. "It's okay, Mama," said my son, "At least you tried." My husband was a little more, well, honest. "This really is lacking taste. What happened?" I posted on Twitter and Facebook and most folks were encouraging. "At least you tried," appeared to be the kindest response, and the most fun one was, "This is why God invented restaurants." And then a few nasty ones: "How can you publicly admit to failing at a dish? You are a cookbook author! You should know better!"

Really?

As a queen of kitchen disasters—and my friends and family will attest to this—I am always cooking up messes. It is part of the program: for any good dish that comes out of my kitchen, there are several that shouldn't have seen the light of day or touched the plates of loved ones.

I once cooked chocolate mousse, and instead of heating the chocolate OVER a pan of water, I added it TO the pan of water. I had a rock solid mousse that no one would touch. Or—and this is the best bad yet—I was using a pressure cooker to make a potato curry. The cooker ran out of water, the whistle blew off its top, and the entire curry spurted out through the cooker's spout and onto the ceiling above. Then some of it fell back onto the stove where a deep frying pan filled with hot oil sat on a burner. The entire thing caught fire, and I almost burnt the house down. It happens, folks.

Failing in the kitchen, or a fear of failing, can be attributed to many things, I suppose: fear of a new cuisine, a new ingredient, fear of showing a loved one we are less than perfect, or fear of creating something inedible. We all know fear, don't we? Fear of being an Indian lady serving Southwestern BBQ, fear of not really understanding how to cut the Super Delicious and Nutritious Pomegranate every damned food magazine keeps touting, or fear of letting your new boyfriend see you are inept in the kitchen ("What if he thinks the same of me in the bedroom?"). Fear exists and is hard to deny.

Perhaps some people feel the pressure to match expectations of being a cook as great as their aunt/mother/father/sister/friend was. That can be hard, I know. My parents are amazing cooks, and I always aspire to be like them. I love, love, love my mother's cooking, and yet nothing I make tastes like hers. I will often complain to her but she reminds me, "It has taken me forty years to learn to cook like this."

Or maybe we are afraid that after one bad meal (the pad thai being my 100th), we will never recover. That one bad meal will set the precedent of all meals—of all things—to come.

This is why God invented the trash can. If it tastes bad, throw it away. I grew up learning to respect food, and wasting it was unthinkable. And most things can be salvaged with the spicy sauce sriracha, so the dump into the trash is infrequent in my house.

Cooking, like anything else, takes practice. While an understanding of ingredients is critical in putting together a dish, it takes trial and error, too. My pad thai lacked sauce—I mean totally. But we moved on.

Failing in the kitchen isn't the real problem as long as you can answer the most important question: what did you learn from it? Failing is a necessary ingredient in cooking success.

The Little Divas

I was about seven, and living in Bahrain, when a young, gorgeous, newlywed Indian woman with a serious UK accent invited me to her house for a "special celebration." It did not sound tempting till she told me I could not only bring friends, but that she would serve my favorite foods.

A few days after accepting this lunch invitation, six of the nosiest, giggliest girls you would ever meet showed up at her house. Barely had we stepped inside when we were asked to remove our slippers and then move onto a large balcony. There, her husband, an eye surgeon, came out with a large steel pitcher in his hand and began to wash our feet. I was mortified. My friends did not seem to care as they giggled and wiggled. Not me. Was he implying we were unclean?

The lady noticed. "Come, Monica, let me dry your feet and then we will eat." I could smell the toasty cumin and hear the sizzle of the bread frying in the wok. It smelled good enough to forgive her husband's thoughtless task. She used a small towel to dry off my wet feet.

We were then asked to sit in a circle and she began to hand out presents—a dozen red bangles, a red stole, and a silver coin. We were restless as she tried to explain the reason for the gifts and the significance of each thing. Where was the wonderful food that we could smell?

She must have sensed it. She went into the kitchen and came back with tiny silver platters filled with black chickpea curry redolent of cinnamon and cloves, golden semolina pudding dotted with sweet raisins and crunchy cashews, deep-fried balloon bread scented with cumin, lentil wafers, a mild homemade mango pickle, and even a bowl of sweetened yogurt.

As we ate the hearty and nourishing meal, she began to tell us a story about Kanjaks. Our group pretended to pay attention as we gobbled as much as our little mouths could hold. Kanjaks—young prepubescent girls—are revered in various parts of India as incarnations of Goddesses. Girls are the very essence of purity and bliss, she said. The washing of the feet, the giving of the gifts, feeding us such a lavish meal—we were being treated like Goddesses, she said.

Recently when I was reminiscing with my mother about how great this lady's food used to be, my mother turned to me, surprised that I had not understood the real meaning of what her friend had been trying to do. In India, where killing a female fetus was considered "normal," and boys were thought of as the more desirable offspring, she was reviving this age-old tradition to give little girls like me true self-esteem. To ensure, I think, in her own way, that when these Kanjaks grew up, they had the same pride about bearing daughters as they did sons.

And I thought I was there for the food.

East Views West

Young teenage girls are supposed to fill their diaries with dreams of love and visions of the valiant princes who would sweep them away from their wicked, curfew-imposing, tightwad, strict, uncool, unhip parents. My diary, however, was filled with the emotions of a kid obsessed with food - particularly the cuisine of the Western Hemisphere. At the tender age of fourteen, I could cook a mean Indian-style leg of lamb, explain how to buy the best hamur (a local fish), smell goat cheese from a mile away, and spell out nine ways to make couscous. But alas, I had never tasted risotto, did not know what rosemary smelled like, and yearned for a taste of asparagus. I knew about Middle Eastern, Indian, and Asian foods, but longed to experience the mysterious West.

My teenage diary, which I found last week, reflects how I learned about Western cuisine from watching sitcoms. When I was growing up in Bahrain (we're actually Indian, but my father worked for one of the oil companies there), there was no

Internet or Amazon.com. The bookstores were tiny and carried local books. My father, who traveled a lot, came home with amazing stories of how the West ate. At home and outside, we ate Asian- or Middle Eastern–inspired food. The only exceptions were from a pizza joint that managed to open and survive and Dairy Queen and Hardees franchises that opened in the late 1980s.

My interest in Western food began when the Middle Eastern television channels finally started showing limited American TV programming for the American armed forces stationed locally. I got my first taste, at age ten, of American TV: *Sesame Street* and *Mr. Rogers*. Although I was old for the content, it was the food-related material that interested me. Quoting from my diary: "Grover made something called a Peanut Butter Sandwich—ask Dad to buy peanut butter."

What was this unique butter that all the kids loved so? Was it sweet or salty, thick or thin? What did they pair it with? So then off we went, Dad and I, to the one small American grocery store to buy this divine peanut butter. One look at the price tag told me it was not going to be. When did I finally taste a peanut butter sandwich? Twenty years later, when my one-year-old asked for a peanut butter sandwich. I had all but forgotten about it. I did taste it. It was an acquired taste.

As I grew older, the local TV channels began to get permission to broadcast more American and British shows. The entries in my diary began to grow like wildfire: "Arnold drinks plain cold milk out of the refrigerator with each meal—*Different Strokes*." That struck me as odd. No Indian mother would let her kids drink cold milk—we had to heat it and add so much stuff to it that it no longer tasted like milk. "Today Dr. Huxtable made Callaloo … what is that? Ask Dad where Jamaica is … and what they eat." I loved the Huxtables and grew up watching them, learning from their eating habits. I was at every Thanksgiving they ever had. The *Facts of Life* crew introduced me to brownies and rye bread. What was a brownie? I had never even heard of it. My dad had. When he went on a trip to Europe, he brought me back some brownies and some Lindt chocolate—to me that is still the best chocolate in the world. Why? Because it was the first Western chocolate I ever tasted and it held in each bite a promise of a cool world. Of course, *Fawlty Towers* and *Some Mothers Do 'Ave 'Em* (British sitcoms) had me yearning for fish-and-chips and quail.

Then came *Dallas* and *Dynasty*. I watched each episode, furiously taking notes on the characters' food habits. They often appeared only to drink and eat what appeared to be fish eggs. Of course, I never saw Joan Collins on screen, just heard her voice—Middle Eastern media rules were very stern. She often wore, I believe, revealing clothes, so each time she came on screen, they would blank her out.

I tasted my first Big Mac at age twenty-one. I had been in the U.S. for twenty-four hours. That was the only thing I wanted to do. It was no small feat for me: a little girl who grew up dreaming of the West had finally made it. McDonald's is such an icon overseas, and my small bite was no small accomplishment.

It has been many years since I wrote that diary, and I have come a long way. I know what truffles are, what terrine is, what foie gras is, and what prosciutto tastes like. I even know what EVOO (extra virgin olive oil) means. I know how to cook a mean meatloaf, and I can make risotto with the best of them. Now, if only I could learn to order a Subway sandwich, I would be all set.

I wrote this piece in 2005 for eGullet.com.

Grocery Store Tales

I went to the grocery store yesterday afternoon. It was a gorgeous day in Northern Virginia. The sun was glittering, a cool wind was blowing, and I was picking up a birthday cake for my little guy. One of the things I love to do at grocery stores, and I am sorry that this will sound weird, is to look at what people are buying and then try to figure out if I can tell their "story" based on their purchases. (If you have seen the movie *Date Night* with Tina Fey, you will know what I am talking about, as the couple in the movie does the same thing with people at restaurants. They like to look at other couples and make up stories. But, I digress.)

So yesterday I was in my merry mood, walking around and looking at people and figuring out what they were up to. A young man was trying to figure out what wine to buy. He looked like he was twelve. He kept pacing up and down the wine aisle. I wondered if it was date night for him and if he was trying to impress someone.

Next was the typical young mom with one kid under her arm, one in the plastic car at the bottom of the shopping cart, and another one in her belly! She was buying—what else?—diapers. Despite being pulled in two different directions by the kids, she was laughing and singing in a language I could not recognize, occasionally bending down to kiss the kids. I wondered where the husband was. Fighting a war? At work as a lawyer? What would she cook him tonight? Or would he cook for her, given that she was about ready to pop?

Then I found this old woman, with a gentle mop of graying hair on her head. She was wearing a large red sweater, black pants, and sensible shoes. She walked slowly, very slowly, which is actually how I got stuck behind her.

She was buying healthy entrees from the freezer section. She had a list that she was having a hard time reading and a harder time crossing off. Her large fingers seemed not to be able to bend. Arthritis? I don't know. Maybe.

I smiled at her.

"I am trying to get all I need to eat this week. It is hard being alone," she said. I just stared. Was she alone in this world? Did no one want to help her? She pulled out another entree and put it in her shopping cart. "I can't cook anymore, not with these hands," she said to me.

She kept going and then came to the ice cream aisle. She picked a few single servings of different ice creams. I followed suit, only picking larger boxes for my kids. "Ah, you have a family," she said. "I only get these for myself."

Then she peeked in my cart and said, "A birthday cake! Who has a birthday today?"

I told her about my son.

"Yes, I thought it was a boy since you had the red car on there!" she said. "He likes cookies? I see you have cookies? I don't eat those any more, not with my teeth. Only ice cream for me at night," she smiled. Then she pointed to all the vegetables in my cart and asked how many kids I had and how I got them to eat vegetables. "I see you like roses," she said, pointing to my flowers.

We began to walk to the checkout counter. "I love looking at people's carts and seeing what they buy," she said. "You can learn so much about them, don't you think?"

You certainly can, ma'am. You certainly can.

How Recipes Are Born

When my German friend, Lydia, made me her favorite childhood dish, Wiener schnitzel, it was more than just a cooking lesson. It was a great lesson in how cultures affect recipes and how recipes reflect our lives.

The first thing I noticed when I entered Lydia's living room was a beautifully framed photograph of her and her Indian husband on their wedding day. Of course, I had to ask: What happens at a Hindu wedding ceremony when a German marries an Indian?

"The hardest part at the wedding," her husband Chandu told me, "was hiding the swastika. In India, it's a popular religious symbol, but I did not want my German in-laws to misunderstand why it was there."

Lydia added that she loved dressing in Indian clothes and jewelry, but found it funny that Chandu's family thought she looked so Indian. "How is that possible?" she said, "I am so very blond."

We were standing in her spacious, spectacularly clean

kitchen.

She began prepping for dinner when her husband returned from work. Tall and lean, he bent down to kiss her. And she smiled. They had met in the early 1990s on her birthday. She was working at the front desk of a Brussels hotel when he checked in. Within eight days of asking her out, he had proposed. She thought he was crazy.

"In a city full of glorious coffee bars and cafes," she reminisced, "he took me to Pizza Hut, of all places, to ask me this question!"

"And when she said no," he added, "I took the Pizza Hut menu and wrote down every phone number in the world where she could reach me—in case she changed her mind."

"Now, we begin," said my German friend, bringing me back to her kitchen. "When I was growing up, we ate Wiener schnitzel whenever we went out. It was our burger and fries. It is served in all family-style restaurants in Germany—comfort food that we loved. It is always served with fries and ketchup."

Whenever her mother made it at home, she told me, they would always serve it with a fresh green salad and lots of cabbage. "We are German; we add cabbage to everything," she laughed and added a handful of grated cabbage to a large bowl of greens. This, I understood, would be our salad for the evening: greens, cabbage, and peppers, to be drizzled with Lydia's homemade dressing of olive oil, balsamic vinegar, coriander, salt, and pepper.

But I was itching for the pièce de résistance for the evening: the schnitzel.

She pulled out a box of pork chops from the fridge. "We will use these. But see, my mother would not like that because they don't have any fat on them. To make the Wiener schnitzel the German way, you need pork with fat! Not lean like I have." She went on to explain that while the traditional dish requires seasoning the meat with salt and then dipping it in egg and bread crumbs and deep-frying, she didn't use eggs or deep-fry.

Instead, she pulled out her secret ingredient—a jar of curry powder.

"Curry powder? In schnitzel?" I asked, surprised.

"My kids have acquired such a spicy palate thanks to their father that when I served schnitzel plain, they weren't too impressed. So I curried it up! And they loved it!"

I asked what the boys would think if they went back to Germany and tasted the schnitzel there.

"They would love the deep-fried version, but I am sure the younger one would remark that the real way to make it is with curry," she said, her sweet laughter filling the air.

She placed the pork on a board and added salt and pepper and a few shakes of curry powder.

Next she took each piece and dredged it in bread crumbs, pressing the meat into the crumbs so it was well covered. A skillet was already on the stove with oil that was beginning to shimmer. In went the pork, and the aroma of curry filled the air.

I could hear her husband in the other room: "Smells divine. Is it done yet?" Lydia checked by pressing down with her finger on the pork. "It is done when it is no longer soft."

And with that, dinner was served. "I made it this way for my mom many years ago," she told me. After that, her mom had returned to Germany with a suitcase full of curry powder.

Our Recipes, Our Lives

This morning I was making a lentil soup for my family almost exactly the way my grandmother in India taught me decades ago. Or so I first thought. Her recipe used six tablespoons of butter, onions, garlic, red lentils, about eight different spices, loads of cilantro, and a touch of salt. I recall my mom making this, but with much less butter, baby peas for us kids, and no salt as Dad was watching his sodium. As I smelled the aroma of garlic from the soup that I was stirring, it occurred to me that my soup today was in truth a reflection of my life here in the U.S., far away from India: butternut squash, chicken stock instead of water, and no cilantro, as my hubby thinks it tastes soapy.

The changes to the recipe had occurred so slowly, so gradually, that I never really noticed that I had changed it. It made me think about all the recipes I made and how, in fact, I had begun to change them to reflect our way of living. At first, I have to admit I felt guilty, almost as if changing the recipe meant I was changing the memory of a childhood taste. Familiar childhood tastes give us a place to belong: they bear witness to our lives. Changing them seemed sacrilegious.

When I told my mother this, she reminded me that she cooked the same way. In fact, I remember that more than thirty years ago, my mother had sat down and jotted some of her favorite recipes in a notebook that I took with me to college.

What I loved in it most was not the recipes, but her notes along the margins: Reduce the chili. Add extra sugar for Monica. Reduce butter because the taste is too greasy.

This could easily qualify as our family cookbook because, in addition to recipes, it holds our memories. My mother lives oceans away, but her cookbook is my constant companion in the kitchen, providing warmth, support, and comfort. In the margins now are my own notes of what my family likes.

But it is not just recipes that get passed down and changed. Even the way food is cooked depends on so many cultural traditions, and they can change as we grow. As each successive generation learns what and how to cook, they often just accept that what they've learned. But then, without even realizing it, they do something different.

It's funny how culture shows up where you least expect it. As I have mentioned before, we never tasted the food as it cooked. To taste the food when you cooked it would make it impure. So I learned how to cook by watching the potatoes brown in heated oil until just tender. I learned to sing a song that was just long enough to perfectly boil eggs. I loved listening to the spices sizzle in hot oil and to smell the herbs as they imparted their aroma in dishes. And now I teach my son to cook the same way—I am always making him smell, touch, and listen to food to learn how to cook it perfectly. But he breaks with "my" tradition: he does love to taste!

When I was growing up, one of my best comfort foods was my father's pièce de résistance: Indian-style scrambled eggs. He would shimmer some oil, throw in onions, tomatoes, green chilies, and cilantro. He would chat with me until the tomatoes softened, then add the eggs and scramble them. The final addition would be turmeric and cayenne. The sweet smell of the onions, the lemony scent of cilantro—I associate them all with my father's love. Not only did I love the recipe, I loved breaking the eggs for him, feeling all grown up when he would let me pluck fresh cilantro from the herb pots, and chatting with him as he cooked. I introduced this dish to my husband and then to my sons.

On a recent visit to India, it warmed my heart to have to wait in line for my father's scrambled eggs behind my boys. As I waited patiently, I heard my husband explain to my dad how much he loved the dish. And then he went on to explain our family rendition of the scrambled eggs—using Indian cheese instead of eggs, mint instead of cilantro, and jalapeños instead of green chilies. Changing a recipe, it turns out, doesn't make it less of an heirloom—in fact, it only makes it more our own.

Sage

Sage is not used in Indian cooking, so you may be surprised to see it here as one of my most favorite ingredients. So let me tell you why it is here—it is one of the very few plants that I cannot kill with my non–green thumb! Sage blossomed in my tiny garden, and I learned to use it in so many different ways—partly because I loved the taste and partly because I was so thrilled it was still growing! Oh, and did I mention that sage in the garden is a sign that the woman rules the house? Need I say more?

I love the taste of sage. It can be a bit bitter sometimes, but it has strong hints of mint and eucalyptus. The flowers of sage plants are edible, too, provided they haven't been sprayed. Sage blossom honey is very delicate in both flavor and color and does not granulate.

My favorite ways to use sage:

1. Fry the individual leaves in some good-quality butter, then use the fried leaves as a garnish for stews, soups, and rice dishes. I make a simple roasted butternut squash soup with sweet potatoes and carrots and garnish it with fried sage—the garnish makes the dish go from simple to spectacular!
2. Add it to your turkey stuffing.
3. Add it to macaroni and cheese for a totally different flavor.

4. Add it to risotto.

5. Add sage and mint to a white tea for a terrific and aromatic herbal tea infusion.

6. Warm some olive oil and add a few sage leaves. Heat on low for about a minute. Remove from heat. Strain and collect the flavored oil. I like to use this oil to cook chicken and also as a base for salad dressings.

7. Pair with cookies and fruit crumbles.

8. Attach a large sage leaf to a slice of veal and prosciutto with a toothpick. Season to your taste, and pan fry with a dash of white wine and shallots for the Italian classic, *saltimbocca alla romana*. The name loosely translates to—*it's so good it jumps into your mouth*!

Food and Family

Save Your Recipes
Before It's Too Late

It was a Monday night, and I had just finished making what felt like my 300th chicken dinner. I was busy developing recipes for magazines and newspapers and food companies, not to mention cooking for my own family. What had once seemed like a dream job now felt like hard labor. And so I did what I always do. I got on the phone.

"You know what? I've got just the thing for you," said my friend after listening to me complain for several minutes. "I want you to go online and order a book called *In Memory's Kitchen*. You can thank me later."

It was, she told me, a collection of World War II–era recipes, and I was a little puzzled as to why she thought this would be helpful. As I started in on my 301st chicken dinner, I went ahead and ordered it anyway. When the book arrived, I lazily paged through it, then sat down and started reading. I didn't put it down until I'd finished—hours later.

To say that the book is a collection of recipes is a serious understatement. It was written by women at the Terezín concentration camp in Czechoslovakia during the Third Reich. These women were eating potato peels and scraps salvaged from garbage piles, but recording from memory recipes for chocolate tortes, roast goose, plum strudel, Bavarian bread, and potatoes with herring. They scribbled their cooking instructions on the backs of propaganda papers passed out at the camp. Writing down their recipes gave these prisoners hope that perhaps someday life would return to normal—if not for them, then for their children or grandchildren.

There is such spirit in those recipes. They made me think about how taste lives on in our minds, how it comforts us in dire times. It caused me to wonder which meals I'll look back on years from now. Which recipes, tedious or simple as they might seem when I am cooking them today for the umpteenth time, will I remember most fondly, and which ones will my kids remember?

I realized then that some of the dishes I loved as a child were virtually lost to me. When I was young, I would travel to India every summer to spend time with my grandparents and our large extended family. Both of my grandmothers died very young, and my memories of them are now fleeting. I struggle to remember how they made the breads and curries that I so loved.

The book renewed my determination to find my paternal grandmother's recipes. Perhaps I would get lucky; perhaps she did write down some notes that were stashed somewhere in her bungalow in Old Delhi. A distant relative had moved into Grandma's house after her death and was still living there, my father said. He offered to drive me there on my next trip to India.

Three months later, I flew with my then five-year-old son Jai from our home in Washington, D.C., to Delhi. I wanted desperately to show Jai the house that held my best childhood memories. We got into the car with my father and, as he drove us to Grandma's old bungalow, I recalled lazy summer Sundays we would spend there while she cooked dinner for the whole family. While I played in the courtyard across from her tiny kitchen, I would watch her diamond nose stud glitter in the summer sun. I could smell the simmering garlicky lentils, the robust chicken curries fragrant with cinnamon and cloves, and hear the sizzle of the potatoes as they hit the hot steel *kadai* pan. Everyone would gather in my grandmother's living room and sit in a circle on the floor to feast on the modest meal, cooked with so much care and devotion. She would lean in to talk to each of us: "See, I made your favorite rice, your favorite curry, your favorite pickle. Now eat some more."

I could barely contain my excitement as the car approached the bungalow—I hadn't been there in almost twenty years—but nothing prepared me for what I saw when my father abruptly stopped the car. There was only rubble in front of us, the skeleton of the place where my childhood home used to be. I was too shocked to cry. We drove back in silence. Later we learned the relative had moved out, and the house had been sold.

Back at my parents' house in Delhi, still numb, I watched my mother cook dinner. She started frying spices and then added lentils and garlic. The kitchen filled with the glorious scents. Then she turned to me: "Come, I am making lamb chops. I have a new spice combination."

"Hold on, Mom. Let me get a pen and paper. I want to write this down."

"Okay, write it down," she said, "but if you want to pass down memories to your son, bring him in the kitchen and make a meal he will remember not only from his palate, but from his heart."

So we called Jai in and assigned him the task of plucking mint leaves off a stem while I began to roast the spices in the skillet, just as I had seen Mom do a million times. I gently moved the skillet from side to side and waited for that moment when the spices relent and fill the air with their aroma. We ground the spices, rubbed the mixture on the lamb and cooked the meat in a hot oven. Dad opened the refrigerator to bring out his own pièce de résistance (he has many although he claims he has only one!): pickled onions—a dish he had re-created from his memories of Grandma's recipe.

Two hours later, we sat in my mother's elegant dining room to eat our dinner of creamy red lentils, vegetable pilaf, lamb chops, chutneys, pickled onions, and cumin-scented potatoes. Meanwhile, a cricket match played on a TV behind us. As we turned to check the score and cheer for the Indian team, the noise level rose a few decibels over insane—a typical scene in my boisterous family.

At that moment, looking at my laughing son across the table eating his lamb, showing off "his mint" and piling his fork with his great-grandmother's tangy onions, I was struck by the true meaning of *In Memory's Kitchen*. It wasn't just about documenting recipes; it was about re-creating the moments behind those meals and celebrating the togetherness and joy food brings. What we eat and how we eat it gives us identity; it helps us define who we are. The women of Terezín never forgot that, and I was sure that now, neither would I.

As we washed the dishes, I hugged my mother, who was bent over the sink. She pulled her soapy hand out of the water and patted me on my face.

"Now," my mother said to me, "what do you want for breakfast tomorrow?"

This story first appeared in Bon Appétit.

The Red Fairy and the
Unending Bowl of Potatoes

I grew up in a house full of girls. So when my first son was born, I was at a loss. How would I mother this miracle? I knew nothing about things boys liked. I was into classical dancing, debates, cooking, reading, writing … But I had no idea how to raise a son

When my first born, Jai, was four, he asked me to tell him my favorite childhood fairytale about an Indian fairy princess, Lal Pari (the Red Fairy), who lived in a golden castle. She had seven brothers whom she loved and took care of.

Of course, there was a witch who tried to lure her away. Lal Pari had a magical pot in which she could make anything her heart desired and the pot never ran out of food. The food in the pot ended only after she ate from it. My son loved to help in the kitchen, could pick out ripe bananas at age two and identify the smell of caramelizing onions at age three, so I thought that perhaps the food-loving Lal Pari would appeal to him.

I learned about Lal Pari when I was about his age. Our family lived outside India, but every summer we would go to our homeland and stay with my grandparents. There was an old lady, a relative, in my grandma's house who would tell me tales of Lal Pari. The old woman made gram flour vermicelli as she told me the stories. Her fingers would make slim noodles and her voice would weave tales of never-ending curries and stews in Lal Pari's food bowl. The old lady and I had nothing in common—she had never been to school, spoke no English, and had never left India. Yet her stories carried me through the summer and became memories and a crucial part of my life. I began sharing the tales with Jai.

My original Lal Pari tales would end with her marrying a prince. Jai loved adding his spin and sometimes the princess would be a doctor—usually a veterinarian—and would end up marrying Shrek. I was grateful that he could take my stories and transform them to his world. I learned from Jai that Lal Pari had a soft spot for Subway sandwiches and that her brothers preferred Five Guys burgers.

Jai grew up and outgrew Lal Pari. And then seven years later, my second son wanted to know about Lal Pari.

Arjun, three, would not add anything to the stories. He would simply listen, often looking lost. And he would ask questions: "Does Lal Pari fly?" "Why does Lal Pari love her family so much?"

It was a Monday night, I remember. I had been away in New York all day and returned home late at night. I heard the boys in Jai's room and stopped to listen at the door.

Jai: "Lal Pari was going out to the market."

Arjun: "*Bhai* (brother), she doesn't just go. Mama said she flies."

Jai: "No, people cannot fly."

Arjun: "But Mama said."

Jai: "Okay, fine. She flew out and there she met Shrek and Lightning McQueen."

Arjun: "No, *Bhai*, Mama said she met her friends at the market. I think Mama is like Lal Pari. When is Mama coming home? I miss her."

I opened the door to the room, and both boys came running toward me. They wanted me to tell them a new Lal Pari story.

I lay down with them and told them about Lal Pari going to the market to buy tomatoes and potatoes and ginger and garlic. She bought long, slender bananas and plump, round apples. Her brothers carried the bags home in their shining new Lightning McQueen car. At home, she made spicy potatoes in her large magical bowl. Of course, Shrek stopped by for dinner with the family. They all sat together at the table, thanked God for the food, and ate as they laughed and played silly games.

I was so busy with my story that I forgot to see if the boys were listening. They had both fallen asleep in my arms.

You know, we all say that life doesn't come with instruction books. I think that is why God made kids. Mine teach me how to love, guide them, and nurture them. In return, I am blessed with watching them bloom and blossom. With Lal Pari and Shrek and McQueen and that never-ending bowl of spiced potatoes.

A Familiar Taste

My mother taught me how to sizzle cumin and how to pound chutneys with a mortar and pestle. She trained me to prepare complex curries scented with cardamom and cinnamon, textured with tomatoes and coriander and bribed with touches of saffron. I inherited her style of *andaza* cooking: estimation cooking where everything is added in pinches and guesses and with a natural sense of an ingredient's role in dish. She wasn't one of those cooks who shied away from eating. Oh, on the contrary, we would cook up a storm and then eat like it was going out of style.

But now, she barely touches food. She has been chronically ill for a decade and fought it all until the medication, finally, took its toll. Her teeth fell out and her taste buds were so damaged that everything tasted sour. My once vibrant and cheerful mother turned into a skeleton with sunken, listless eyes.

My family tried all kinds of new foods to lure her to try something: *Here is a kiwi, try this red pear, here is a new drink.*

Nothing enticed her.

One day, feeling defeated, I made simple potatoes sizzled with cumin. I placed it in front of her, ready to hear, "Take this away."

Instead, she said, "Do you remember when I first taught you to make these? You would cut the potatoes in all different sizes and they never cooked right! You used so much oil that you practically drowned the cumin." And then she picked up a small piece and put it in her mouth.

"This tastes so good, just like I remember," she said and ate two more pieces. It was the first time in weeks she had eaten more than a bite of anything.

I realized she was living in memory's kitchen and that is what we needed to feed her: foods that brought back memories of a kinder and happier time in her life. And hope that those memories would make her want to eat again, a bite at a time.

Counting Peas

As a very young child, my son Jai had an unaccountable aversion to learning any language other than English. Yet I was determined to teach him Hindi, my mother tongue, to ensure he did not miss out on a culture and heritage for lack of simple knowledge of its language.

I would point to his clothes, toys, and books and encourage him to respond with their Hindi names. Eventually, he spoke a few words—he could point to a chair and call it *kursi* and say the numbers from one to ten in Hindi. But he did not know simple phrases such as "How are you?" or "My name is Jai." He could not have a conversation in Hindi.

That all changed during a trip to India when Jai was four. I was sitting with my mother on the floor, shelling peas. As we were laughing and talking, Jai wandered over, picked up a pea pod with great curiosity and asked what it was. "It is *mattar*," my mother told him. "Peas?" he wondered. "Inside this?" He loved the fact that he could open the pod and find a treasure.

He opened one, then another and another. He sat still, which in itself was an achievement. He began to listen to us, to ask questions.

Some mothers like to color with their young children, some read books, some watch television. I could never have imagined our time together would be used to shell peas.

Once we were back in the States, I searched supermarkets and farmers' markets for peas in pods. I rinsed them, patted them dry, and waited for three o'clock so I could pick up Jai from school and we could shell peas. When pea pods were hard to find, I cheated, more than once, passing off edamame as peas. Rarely were we able to eat the peas for dinner. By the time Jai's tiny fingers got them out of the pods, they were too squished or had gone straight into his mouth. I didn't care as long as we sat and shelled and talked.

We sat on the floor and started by sorting the pea pods, his fingers working furiously to separate the little baby pods from the mother pods and the daddy pods. Some days we named the piles of pods for his school friends—Zack, Sam, Casey. Then we counted. Jai could count to 20 in Hindi by then and finished counting in English. On a few occasions, we reached 30 together.

Then came Jai's favorite part, the time for me to tell him stories—in Hindi. We always started with the story of the witch, the one who would come and make a home in your hair if you went out without drying it on a cold day. The story would somehow segue into what Buzz Lightyear or Spider-Man would do if he found this witch. (An interesting question, since we could not find a bit of hair on either of their heads.) Each story had a different ending, depending on which action figure was stationed next to Jai for the afternoon.

After the witch would come the story of an Indian princess who lived in a golden castle. I wanted it to end with her marrying a handsome prince. My son, however, would add his four-year-old's spin and American viewpoints. Sometimes the princess would be a doctor—usually a veterinarian—and would end up marrying Shrek. Other times, the gentle princess would be transformed into a superhero and I was pleasantly challenged to come up with the Hindi names for laser guns and robotic evildoers.

One day, Jai asked me, "Mom, *apne kahania kaha see seekhi?*"

Where did I learn the stories? Why, from Bahenjee, of course.

By now Jai knew that word meant "older sister," and his curiosity was piqued since I had no older sister. She was not related to me, I explained. It was a term often used as a mark of respect for an older person. A distant relative by marriage, she lived in a quiet part of my *dadi*'s house in Delhi. Dadi, my father's mother, lived in what most people refer to as an Indian bungalow that housed a joint family—14 people on an average day, not including the various relatives who would show up out of the blue.

With her crooked teeth, thinning white hair, flowing white sari, and shrill voice, Bahenjee lived on the fringes of Dadi's household. She had her own small area—steel *almirah* or armoire, *charpai* or cot—and wildly painted loud pictures of various gods on the mostly bare and peeling wall. On a shelf were statues of gods, incense sticks, fresh jasmine flowers, silver coins. Bahenjee generally rose at an ungodly hour—4:00 a.m.— and did the work of an alarm clock for the house, singing prayers tunelessly at the top of her voice.

"*Ab who kaha hai?*" asked Jai. Where is she now?

I had no idea.

"*Nanu se poochege?*" He pointed to the phone for me to call his grandfather in India to ask him. I did, and my father told us that after my grandparents died, Bahenjee went to live with her son. She had since died.

Jai asked me more and more about her and her stories, and the memories came flooding back.

On my summer vacations, when I was a child, I would look forward to going to Dadi's house so I could be with Bahenjee, for she was one of the best storytellers in the world. You and I shell peas, I told Jai; Bahenjee and I would make *sev*—noodles— as she shared stories. We would sit together in the hot Delhi sun after her ritual of sweeping the concrete courtyard with a wooden broomstick, brushing away dust and dirt I couldn't see and laying out a bamboo mat, or *chitai*, for us to sit on. She would spread newspapers in front of the mat and peel a few Indian oranges, or *santras*, for me to eat. Then she would bring out the chickpea dough.

Bahenjee would make small logs of the dough, and she taught me how to hold each one between my fingers as if I were counting the beads of a rosary. Away we would go, preparing small bits of sev as princesses crossed paths with evil witches. Even as she talked, Bahenjee outpaced me in making sev. She would go through containers of dough while I was still struggling with my first log. She never seemed to notice that I generally made a mess and seemed to be interested only in the stories. Occasionally, she would ask me to wet a muslin cloth to cover the dough as it started to dry up. We would sit in that glowing Delhi heat for hours and I would listen, mesmerized.

As I recalled Bahenjee's stories for Jai, it occurred to me that the tales she had told me had been in Multani—a dying language I learned through her stories. All of the stories were set in my father's birthplace, Multan—a part of India until the separation of India and Pakistan. Bahenjee spoke Hindi, the more colloquial language, as well, but seemed to prefer telling the stories in her own language, stopping to translate only if I looked totally lost. She would recount painfully how she was forced to leave her motherland. She would talk about my father's childhood, about her own family, about the food and the festivities.

Her language connected me to a place I would never see and a culture I had never known. No one in my family ever returned to Multan. Bahenjee chronicled a history that was lost in a war over religion and hate. I learned prayers and nursery rhymes in Multani.

Bahenjee's stories ended, inevitably, when the dough did. I have always wondered what she did in the winters.

Learning to appreciate another culture through its language, through the words of an old woman who had seen life and lived to tell about it, now feels like a blessing. When my parents told us their childhood stories, we rolled our eyes. It always seemed to be intended as a lecture, prefaced with, "When I was your age …" Bahenjee's stories were different. They transported me, intrigued me.

Several years have gone by since Jai and I started counting peas. At the age of eight, he speaks Hindi, though not flawlessly. Often he mixes English and Hindi words to create his own language. He has even picked up a few stray words of Multani.

Now, the questions he asks in his Hindi-English mix are no longer simple. *Kya sab log bad hai?* Are all people bad?

Why are those soldiers carrying *banndooks*, guns?

Why do people die, will I die? *Aap bhi?* Will you?

Jai no longer struggles with the language; now it's my turn. I struggle for the right words, the right answers, in any language.

This essay first appeared in The Washington Post*'s Style section several years ago, and was nominated for an IACP award.*

A Deep Red

Wine is a mystery to me—I don't understand all its nuances, but I revere it, and it has always held a special place in my heart. Choosing the right type of wine, I am told, is an art: the wine should be in perfect harmony with the food it is served with.

Sometimes, though, it's about more than just the palate.

A few years ago, my husband and I visited my uncle in the Austrian Alps. We were on vacation and decided to spend a few days with him and his wife. I had never met her and had not seen him in over thirty years.

He had left India at age twenty; I was about a year old then. He now ran a pension nestled in the heart of the Zell Am See, just outside of Salzburg. An Indian king had once remarked that the Kashmir valley reminded him of heaven on earth; Zell Am See begged the king's claim—a stunning valley adorned with nature's best gifts. Cows grazed in the emerald pastures on hills studded with yellow-hued flowers. Tiny houses that looked almost like doll houses lined the roads. It was so tranquil—even the sounds of the cars seemed strangely in harmony with nature. An amber sun ready to scatter vermillion rays had just begun to set. The valley reminded me of the perfect postcard pictures of the Alps on the covers of tiny Lindt chocolates I had eaten as a child. It was heaven on earth.

We had arrived on a cool, crisp May morning, and we spent the day hiking and sightseeing in the city. He asked that we be home in time for aperitifs.

We returned from the hike famished and thirsty. He must have sensed it and immediately led us outside onto the deck. He had laid a beautiful setting with appetizers, wines, and pretty white embroidered Indian napkins. The weather had cooled even more, and there was a slight chill in the air. I sat and accepted the glass of wine he poured for me. The atmosphere seemed a bit awkward—though related by blood, we lived in separate parts of the world and were practically strangers.

"Overwhelming" was the word that came to mind as I sipped the wine offered to me so graciously. I am not sure if it was the heady sensation from the strong-tasting wine or my uninitiated palate, but a strange thought came into my mind. My father had once told me about an Indian queen whose skin was so translucent that when she drank wine, it showed through her veins. My neck was surely not translucent, but the wine was so deep red I wondered if it showed through.

It is Indian etiquette to drink what your host offers you— and so I did politely, gasping with each sip. The woodsy wine played devils' songs down my gullet. I am not much of a wine drinker and the wine made me a bit edgy. I even worried about getting drunk on an empty stomach in front of strangers and this strong red—a merlot—did not help. But the hand that poured the wine seemed so gentle and hospitable, I felt it ill-mannered to ask for a different drink. The deep red consumed my attention as I observed it in the finely cut crystal glass. How could something so beautiful taste so unfriendly? My lack of taste was clearly not shared by my husband. He seemed to cherish each sip, oblivious to my questioning glances.

Baby pink onions mounded over thick slabs of smoky sausages, puff pastry filled with strongly spiced minced lamb, small potato-and-onion-stuffed bread wedges, and lime pickle set on the table seemed to fight with the wine to gain the upper hand.

I remembered my uncle only through the stories my maternal grandmother—his mother—shared with me about his youth back in India. I recalled the most colorful one and shared it at the table. He was seventeen at the time, she said, and it was a big day. He was sitting for the entrance exam to a very prestigious college. She had waited by the door all afternoon for his return. When she saw him, her pounding heart calmed down. He was smiling. "I did great Mama," he yelled, "great—I will pass with flying colors." She hugged and kissed him and let him go out with his friends. When the test results came, he had failed the exam—miserably at that—she said. She was mad: why had he not told her? "Simple," he said, "if I had told you then, I would have gotten yelled at twice!"

We laughed. The ice was finally broken.

My uncle's eyes softened when he turned to me and his voice became gentler. I am a mirror image of my mother and I suspect I reminded him of her, his sister. "Eat," he prodded, just as his mother used to, "take some more. You haven't touched the food."

He fed us until we could eat no more and served more wine. I quietly sipped the wine as I listened to him reminisce about how his only memory of me was holding me as a baby. The wine seemed to get gentler, fruitier.

It turned out to be a long night. After all, we had thirty years to catch up on.

He signaled for more wine. I found myself nodding yes. It was beginning to grow on me. We reminisced about Delhi, our birthplace.

The last toast of the night was his. "To my family," he said simply. "To my family." His eyes—hazy with tears—said the rest. We drank the deep red. I had stopped fighting it, and it had rewarded me kindly. A warm spicy flavor now teased my tongue. Our conversation appeared to take the lead from the wine—a bit awkward at first, then warm, and finally inviting and familiar.

Years later at an Indian restaurant, I am debating over a drink with dinner. It's a special night. We are meeting some strangers who I am hoping will become new friends. I glance at the wine list, and there it is. There it is, on the menu—my deep red friend.

The sommelier politely questions my choice of wine. "Madam, this red? Perhaps a lighter wine for your spicy meal? A red may not be just perfect." he says.

"But it really is," I say. "It really is."

Why I Don't Cook for My Parents

Mussels cooked in a saffron-coconut stew, shrimp fritters with just the right crispness, chicken kebabs laced with brandy—these are dishes I tell my dad about all the time. They are my passion—my creations as a food writer. He often advises me on the recipes, telling me what to add, what to change, what to increase, and what to substitute. I listen, because my dad is one of the best home cooks I know.

Just a few months ago, he and I were discussing our favorite chicken curry recipe that shines with flavors of green and black cardamom. I love the way he makes it, and we were discussing changing the texture of the onions. He is in Delhi, and I am in Washington, D.C., and these discussions form the crux of our conversations. Yet in our last talk something was different. Dad kept asking when I was going to cook all these dishes for him.

Strangely, I rarely cook for my parents. It isn't because I am afraid to or because I feel that they won't like my dishes or that they will complain or that my dishes won't be up to their standards. It isn't any of these things at all.

I grew up nourished in spirit by my father's travel stories involving food and my mother's unerringly mouthwatering dishes. His stories evoked a world of Irish pubs, French bistros, Indian curry houses, Swiss chalets, and Austrian pensions that I had never seen; my mother's hand created perfectly spiced dishes without ever holding a measuring cup, spoon, or bowl. She was always adding a little of this and a little of that to create memorable dishes. My sister and I would take turns doing dinner chores. Then we would spend time around the dinner table talking about our day, about life in general, or about the cost of okra, but always together.

I left home when I was seventeen and wandered the world: first, college; then marriage; then babies; and somewhere in there ... careers. I grew up in the Middle East, my parents settled in India, and I settled in the U.S. When I visited them, I just wanted them to cook for me. I longed for my mother's crisp fried okra, my dad's cardamom-scented oatmeal, or the best dish of all—having both of them in the kitchen discussing and making a mutton curry. I love that they have been married for more than forty years and have possibly been making that same curry for that long, and yet they always discuss how to make it and what to do.

Rarely will I volunteer to cook my creations for them. I tell them about my food, and they cook from my cookbooks, but when I am there with them in their home, I don't cook for them. I was raised on their food—it is the memory and the home of my childhood. While they may miss my chicken kebabs, I know they don't long for them as I do for my father's butter chicken.

I cook for my own children in the hope that I will create similar memories. I cook for my kids in the hope that when they go off into the big, wide world, the memory of their mother's chicken curry, the scent of her caramelized onions with garlic, the whiff of her cinnamon-scented rice pudding will tug at their heart and bring them back home—just like my parents' cooking does for me.

A version of this was published on NPR.org.

Bird of Paradise

The prep work always began on Thursday night.

In 1980, when I was ten, we lived in the Middle East, and Thursday was the start of the weekend. I'd huddle with Dad in our small galley-style kitchen as he began making butter chicken: a glorious dish of chicken pieces marinated in yogurt, cumin, fenugreek, ginger, and garlic, oven-roasted and cooked in a sinful, creamy butter and tomato sauce.

"The first thing is the chicken," he would say. "If the chicken is not of good quality, you can forget the dish. The frozen chicken on the market is no good." Working closely with his butcher—my father still has a closer relationship with his meat vendors than most people have with their doctors—he would pick out the best chicken and have it chopped up his way.

Dad began the marinade in a bowl filled with homemade yogurt in which he swirled his long, slender fingers to gently whip it. "Yogurt is the key. It tenderizes the chicken, it makes it soft," he said. "People forget that."

My father is an engineer by trade. When my sister and I were young and we lived in Bahrain, he traveled constantly and was often gone for long periods of time. After a day at school, I'd wait for his return—rather irrationally—by the large windows of our cozy family room each night.

When he finally came home—from Beirut, Dubai, Alabama, Delhi, London, Kuwait, or Paris—he brought gifts of unusual foods, such as tinned baked beans with bacon, Lindt chocolates, and dates stuffed with pistachios. However, when he asked, "What would you like to eat this weekend?" the answer was always the same: butter chicken.

After the yogurt came tablespoons of melted clarified butter and a large squeeze of lemon juice, then a slathering of canned pureed tomatoes. "This is the real butter chicken," he'd say. "I can tell you it tastes like the one from Moti Mahal restaurant in Delhi. Did I ever tell you that is where this dish originated? I will take you there when we are in Delhi next. We can eat and sit outside on the lawn and listen to beautiful *ghazals* [Urdu poetry]."

As the memories of Moti Mahal filled his mind, he would begin to recite poetry by Indian legends. I understood nothing because I spoke no Urdu, yet his soothing, deep voice kept me entranced as he sang and cut slits into the chicken so the marinade would be absorbed. Then he added the chicken to the marinade, rubbing it until it seemed as though the chicken was born with the mixture on. The chicken needed to marinate overnight. And I needed to go to bed.

The next morning, I would be up with him at eight, ready to go to the market to buy tomatoes for the curry. Years later, when he visited me in the States, he was appalled I went to the grocery store once a week. "You buy tomatoes now for use on Friday? They won't be fresh. What is the point?"

Once, after returning from London, Dad did not stop talking about chicken tikka masala—a British version of butter chicken. "It had onions. Who puts onions in butter chicken? I found out that it was originally created using a can of tomato soup? Soup in making butter chicken? Who does that?" The rant took several years to die down.

His hands reached out to the spice cabinet for the treasures that made the dish sparkle. "Smell this *methi*, child—here, smell," he said. "When I was a kid, my mother would make it, and it made the whole kitchen smell like paradise. Moti Mahal did not add this to their chicken dish. They should have." I leaned over and pretended to smell the dried herb, which smells like maple syrup, all the while reveling in the precious time with my father.

He'd place the chicken pieces single file on a foil-lined sheet to roast in the oven as we began preparing the sauce. First he would fish out his ancient grinder. He made me smell the pungent ginger, and he laughed as I scrunched my long nose at the garlic. Both went into the grinder with fiery green chiles to make the paste.

It was time to cook. Butter would go into a hot *kadai*, a large, steel wok-shaped pot, as he would regale me with stories of his college days or how he agreed to marry Mom without even seeing her first. In went the paste and the fresh tomatoes. He would stir, pause, analyze, stir, and use the back of his spoon to mash the tomatoes. Then he stopped and pulled the roasted chicken from the oven.

"Now is the secret nobody knows," he would say as he pointed to the pan. "This marinade has all the flavors from the spices and the chicken. This is what makes the masala real." He tilted the marinade into the wok. I watched him smile, frown, and finally look at peace as the tomatoes cooked to his satisfaction, and the oil moved out toward the sides of the wok. Then he added the chicken and cooked it until all the flavors melded.

My job came at the end. I gently cut the side of a plastic pouch of heavy cream and poured it into the chicken. The dish was complete. And it was time to invite everyone to eat.

Years later, my son asked me to make butter chicken for him. Reluctantly, I did. He tasted it and declared, "It is really good, Mom, but his is better." Ah, the relief I felt. I still need my dad to show me how.

This was first published in the Washington City Paper.

The Indian Wedding Feast,
a Modern Marvel

November 27, 2003 was a day Hindu astrologers picked as auspicious. On that day, India's capital city of New Delhi hosted 14,000 weddings. It hosted the same number again for the next two days in a row!

Today's urban Indian weddings are a picture of national and international integration. In earlier times, brides and bridegrooms would be of the same caste, perhaps from the same geographic state and most assuredly of the same religion. Modernization of thought and tradition, socioeconomic factors, and a prosperous middle class have changed this. And nowhere are these changes more evident than in the wedding feasts. From exotic to traditional, from regional to international, the wedding banquets are truly spectacular.

Armed with every single piece of formal clothing I owned, I attended a week-long, fifteen-event family wedding in Delhi, culminating with the wedding ceremony itself on that very lucky day. Wedding guests, flying in from five continents, swelled to the thousands. (Wedding invitations are often addressed to family, friends, and even friends of friends. The hosts consider it an insult if you do not bring along a huge group to the wedding.)

Breakfasts, lunches, and dinners were seamlessly coordinated for hundreds of people and their chauffeurs and servants. Each event—sometimes there were four a day—required a unique feast and décor—not to mention new outfits, shoes, diamonds, and other finery for those attending these celebrations. The menus were dictated by the religious theme of the event or the whim of the bride. Chefs and cooks were ferried in from other cities in India, along with their own mobile kitchens, *haandis* (cooking vessels), enormous tandoors (clay ovens) and troupes of helpers.

The festivities for this Hindu wedding began at the bride's home on Saturday, November 22 (five days before the wedding) with a prayer ceremony. Hindu scriptures dictate the food for this occasion be free from garlic and onion (known in ancient times as aphrodisiacs) to maintain its purity. The vegetarian menu featured more than thirty choices, ranging from velvety tomato soup tempered with mustard seeds to a creamy pea and almond curry.

The next three nights seemed like one long endless party. At "cocktail dinners" you had your choice of eight different pastas (farfalle to fettuccine) with five different toppings, served with one of four different sauces (spinach, mornay, mushroom, or arrabbiata).

A more adventurous cocktail menu featured the Swiss specialty, rosti: potatoes were shredded, sautéed until golden brown, and served with generous amounts of cheese. At another station at the same party, lovers of Indian food could sample *kathal biryani*, a rice dish layered with curried jackfruit, or *dal khushk Punjabi*, a creamy combination of lentils simmered for more than eight hours. Or (ignoring Dr. Atkins) a guest could head straight to the bread counter for a choice of cumin, mint, butter, or even chocolate-laced Indian breads prepared in the tandoor by chefs flown in from the Indian city of Meerut.

The morning of the day before the wedding began with a women-only ritual called *kwar dhoti*. The bridegroom's sister visited the bride's family with gifts for the bride, including a cup of henna and the first outfit to be worn right after the wedding. For this event, a chef flew in from Punjab to make his specialties: *makkai ki roti* (Indian-style corn bread) prepared on a griddle and *sarson ka saag* (pungent mustard greens), both served with homemade white butter on the silver platters each guest received as a party favor.

The night before the wedding is reserved for the tradition of henna. The natural dye is used to paint intricate designs on the bride's hands and legs. The myth is that the depth of the color of henna on your hand determines the depth of your mother-in-law's love for you! It is the bride-to-be's last night at home. Traditionally, a mother ensures that her daughter's favorite dishes are on the menu that night, so we enjoyed deep-fried lotus stem, black chickpeas in a spicy brown sauce served with piping hot Indian balloon bread, warm carrot fudge, and cardamom-scented tea.

The wedding, after four ritual-filled events earlier that day, finally arrived. A red-and-gold royal pavilion with lavish seating, gorgeous floral arrangements, buffet tables, silk-draped reception areas, bars, and dessert lounges had been custom-built on a fifty-acre farm. The bride, dressed in a deep red Indian gown studded with Swarovski crystal, and the groom in a cream Nehru-collar suit, wed in front of 1,500 guests on a stage adorned with more than 5,000 flowers. Four, six-foot-long tables were covered with nine different types of Indian dough balls ready for the oven, to be baked fresh at the requests of the guests. Pasta, Mongolian, Mexican, Indian, Continental, and Chinese cooking stations provided ample choices. A twenty-gallon terra cotta pot on a slow flame brewed milk laced with cashews, almonds, pistachios, saffron, and sugar—the choice drink in the bone-chilling Delhi weather.

After the wedding feast came the wedding reception. For the first time in seven days, the menu featured alcohol and non-vegetarian food. The rush to the teppanyaki cooking station with grilled Japanese food and the salad bar with more than twenty types of salads cued me into what was hot that night. The dessert table served *chuski* (an Indian version of Italian ice laced with sugar syrup), mille-feuille (the French dessert of puff pastry and cream), chocolate truffle cake, and apple strudel. Of course, when fourteen cases of Scotch, twelve cases of wine, and four cases of tequila are consumed in one night, you can safely assume your guests had a happy night.

As we began to leave the reception, I noticed the mouth freshener table. Yes, the final tables offered the departing guests a sweet token of thanks—thirty-five types of mouth fresheners—and the caterer was still adding more choices.

This story first appeared in The Washington Post.

Is the Food Better If the Kitchen Is Glamorous?

Some people envy their neighbors' diamonds or cars. I am a closet coveter of other people's kitchens. You know the kitchens I am talking about—with Sub-Zero refrigerators, silicone basting brushes, a breakfast "nook" that seats twenty, Lenox dinnerware for fifty, double convection ovens, six-burner cook-tops with grills, and the ever-so-important touch-free trash cans.

Since I spend every free minute in the kitchen, I have always dreamed of having a gourmet cooking paradise—the inspiration for flawlessly executed meals, where every nook and cranny personifies culinary class, and every appliance takes your breath away.

The first time I saw one of these magnificent citadels of culinary superiority, I was living in Cleveland. Some new friends had invited my husband and I to dinner. To say the house was enormous would be an understatement. As our hostess guided us through the house, I was hoping for a possible tour of the kitchen. Instead, she led us straight to the living room.

As the food began to arrive, perfectly plated on tableware that would make the King of Brunei jealous, my curiosity began to grow. I had to see the kitchen where this gorgeous feast was being prepared. So I excused myself on the pretext of looking for the powder room, and wandered into the kitchen.

I think I turned every shade of green—from spring pea to avocado—as I entered the kitchen with its hardwood floors and granite countertops. My own kitchen at the time got crowded if two people entered and seemed as if it belonged in a dollhouse. This kitchen could hold an entire Mardi Gras celebration and still have room left over.

Perfectly crafted knives with mother-of-pearl handles sat in the center of the island. I picked them up and caressed them longingly.

"Ah, there you are," said my friend, startling me.

"I was just admiring these knives," I said, each word dripping with wanting.

"I got those when I got married," she replied, "fifteen years ago."

Fifteen years? These knives looked brand new. I let it pass. I continued on my tour of her kitchen. There would never be any need to exercise if I owned a kitchen like this. I could easily cover a mile just walking around.

"Come on," said my hostess, pulling my arm and removing a tray from the oven. "Let's eat."

We walked back into the dining room and had dinner. The food was perfect, and I knew it was because of the gorgeous kitchen.

As we were leaving, my husband pointed quietly through the open kitchen door to stacks of takeout boxes perched atop the sparkling stainless-steel trash can.

Our hostess noticed and laughed. "I hate to cook," she said. "I just order out."

The Ghosts of Cakes Past

I don't bake. Let me clarify that: I cannot bake. I did not grow up in a house where anyone baked. Until I came to the U.S. and had kids, I had never baked a cookie. Ever. My mother and her mother—or for that matter anyone in our house—never baked. The only "oven" I knew was a small tandoor (clay oven) we used to roast meats. But baking? Never. We went to the closest bakery to buy our double roti (white, sliced bread), fruitcakes, and the occasional fresh cream pineapple cake. I grew up around the enticing scent of cardamom-and-saffron-spiced curries, charcoal-smoked kebabs, and fried milk desserts—but never the smell of a freshly baked cake.

Usually, when I am upset, I try to cook. When I have a decision to make, I go in the kitchen and lose myself in my spices, in the sizzle of the hot oil, in the smell of the sautéing ginger, in the rumble of the boiling rice. And yet today, as I am faced with a very difficult decision, I decide to bake. A cake, no less!

I am not sure what I am doing here, surrounded by flour, eggs, butter, brown sugar, vanilla. I stare at them, and all the ghosts of cakes past stare back. They are laughing at me. The overcooked and burned cake I made a year ago, the chocolate soufflé that never rose, the three-tier cake that ended up in the trash, the cookies that could change the game of hockey forever: edible pucks, anyone? A chill runs down my spine as I recall all the bad decisions I have made in the past. What if this time is no different?

I am torn about what to cook.

I stare at the familiar yellow turmeric. The powder in the small transparent bottle looks like warm sunshine on sunny day. The cumin calls my name. The cinnamon beckons to be added to the lamb in my fridge.

I close the spice cabinet.

I am going to bake a cake. God help us all.

I begin by reading the instructions and can almost hear cookbook author Nancie McDermott talking to me. I met her at a conference this year. Her vibrant spirit and her contagious laughter attracted me to her. I am cooking from her book. Perhaps I have decided to bake because I am trying to channel her and have her here with me. She looks like the kind of person who could make hard decisions easily.

Not me.

I begin by opening the bag of flour. It spills all over the counter and the floor. The fine white powder covers the newly cleaned hardwood floor. I want to clean it up. Instead I simply stand there. It is how I feel. My spirit is covered in dust, and I cannot seem to shake it off.

I bend down and clean the floor. But it seems I have just made a bigger mess. Funny how it seems like my life now. I plug one hole to have another one open up.

I begin to read the instructions again and they say to boil some milk and butter. I can do that. I think. The weight of my decision is hurting me so much that I cannot function. I hear the kids in the living room playing a game of carom. It is a fun game. It is like playing pool except it is on a flat board and there are little "coins" instead of balls and instead of a cue, there is a larger coin called a striker to strike them with.

The kids hear me rattling around the kitchen, and come to see what all the fuss is about. The older one offers to break the eggs in a container so I can proceed with this monumental dish. He looks at the recipe photo; it is stunning, "Wow, Mom. This looks amazing. Look at all the caramel on this cake!"

Oh, right, have I mentioned that I have never made caramel icing before?

He breaks the eggs as I stand and watch him. I haven't created too many amazing things in my life but he is one of the best ones yet. He smiles at me. "You look tired," he says and then begins to help me clean the floor.

I stand back and watch him. He is cleaning while his four-year-old brother is standing there, quietly, throwing more flour on the floor. They make me laugh, these little miracles.

They run back to their game, and I begin to continue my cake or what I hope will be a cake.

As the milk and the butter meld together on the stove, I begin to look for the cake pans. I know I have them somewhere. I begin to look in earnest for the pans. I spot an old plate a friend had given me, an old jar that hosted a shrimp pickle I once made, and a broken spatula that holds heavy memories.

How did I get myself into this mess? Why do I have to make this decision? Why can't decisions make themselves? Better yet, why can't things go back to the way they were, when we were all strangers to each other, when there was no familiarity, when there was no relationship, when there was nothing that could hurt? I am struggling with a relationship that needs to end. I don't want to end it. I can't end it. But I have to end it. When something is a source of constant pain, it is time to let go. But I can't. I am holding onto it, praying it will get better; instead, it is getting worse.

My husband of eighteen years wanders into the kitchen. I want to go and hug him. He knows I am struggling with this decision. He comes over and hugs me and as gently and kindly as possible whispers, "Don't worry. Don't try so hard. Let it be." I know he is right. But I don't feel it yet. I am not ready to let it be.

He leaves to watch a football game. I return to my hunt for the cake pans.

Much to my dismay, I find the pans.

This means I will have to go on.

I sift; I measure; I pretend to know what I am doing. I have been doing that all year. Pretending.

I cannot pretend anymore; I am no good at it. I am stuck between a rock and a hard place, and only the right choice will help me.

What is the right choice? How does one know when a decision will heal and when it will hurt more?

I don't know. I seem to be saying and writing that a lot lately: I don't know.

My four-year-old complains about that. He asks how planes fly, why the wind only blows on our face when the windows are down in the car, how plants eat, how the little people get inside the TV, why the sky is blue, why the grass is green, why butter is so delicious and why rice can be red. I say I don't know. Then I hug him. I am tired. The choices I have to make have made me tired. But he makes me laugh as he makes up answers to his own questions.

He comes in and stares at the baking cake in the oven through the little glass window in the door. We smile at each other. A sweet, warm smell has filled my tiny kitchen. A reassurance, that there is peace to be found in the small things in life.

He runs off to find his brother.

I begin to make the caramel icing. I read the instructions again. I can do this. The brown sugar, the butter, the milk begin to fall in love with each other in my pan and meld together to become a gorgeous brown crème.

The cake has cooled on the rack and does not look like a volcano exploded. In fact, it looks like a fairly decent pound cake. Nancie would be proud. Perhaps it is too early to say that. No one has tasted it yet.

I need a spatula to spread the icing. I cannot find it and as I peek in the pan on the stove, I notice the icing hardening.

I sit down and stare at the kitchen. It is a mess. I am a fairly clean cook, and yet today I have made it look like my husband was cooking, unsupervised.

I make myself some coffee and sip it as I taste the cake, hardened icing on the side.

Did I really do it? Did I just bake a two-tier cake with almost-icing on it?

My eyes are moist. I have wandered through unknown territory and come out the other end. Mostly unscathed.

I still don't know what I am going to do. But then, perhaps, that is the point. I don't have to know. It is like my younger son and his questions. My husband and I never seem to have adequate answers, and yet he trusts us. He makes up his own sometimes. But more importantly, he trusts that we will guide him to the right answers when the time is right.

I have to trust that things will work out as they are meant to be.

Perhaps some people are only meant to be in our lives at a certain time and not at another. It does not mean that friendships are lost or lives have to be ruined. It is just time to move on. Trusting in the process is hard; believing that the right answer will come out the other end is harder.

And yet, here I am with a gorgeous caramel cake, a family that is praising my nonexistent baking skills, and a feeling that everything is going to be just fine.

This story was included in Best Food Writing 2014, *edited by Holly Hughes.*

Fennel Seeds

I love fennel seeds. They have hints of anise and even a touch of green cardamom. Fennel seeds look very similar to cumin seeds, but are slightly bigger and green in color. They are highly aromatic and used in cultures around the world. In India, they are used in curries, breads, and drinks. Raw fennel seeds are said to aid digestion, which is why you'll often see a bowl of them by the door of Indian restaurants.

In Italy, fennel is used to flavor cured meats. It is said that in ancient Rome, Pliny the Elder "called for them to be chewed to wake the mind and relieve flatulence"! Chinese five-spice powder uses fennel as one of its ingredients, as do some blends of herbes de Provence.

My favorite ways to use fennel:

1. Add to your favorite risotto or rice pilaf recipe.
2. Pair with baked fish for a delicately aromatic dish.
3. Mix fennel seeds into bread dough before baking for a surprising flavor and crunch.
4. Eat raw to freshen your breath and help with digestion.
5. Gently toast the seeds and then grind along with black pepper, cumin, and coriander seeds for an aromatic rub for fish.
6. Add to your lemonade for an aromatic twist to the drink.

Food and Love

Fasting for Love, Part 1

It was the intention that counted.

Karva Chauth, an Indian fasting custom that takes place in October or November, has always fascinated me. Each year as I was growing up, I would wait for it so that I could watch my mother perform all its rituals.

As a child, I would hide behind the door and observe her as she got ready for the occasion. Each year on *Karva Chauth*, she would get up early. I could hear her and my father cooking up a storm in the kitchen. Around four-thirty in the morning, she would eat *puri* (fried bread) and *aloo* (potatoes) and drink a cup of tea. While my father went off to work, my mother began her fast. The fast would last all day and required complete abstinence from eating or drinking. In the Hindu religion, this was a day for her to pray for her husband's long life.

I loved the evenings, when it was time for her to break her fast. She would dress in all her finery, and then ready her prayer plate (this is a beautiful plate filled with flowers, special desserts, a small terra cotta lamp and other things used during the prayers). We would all head over to a friend's home for the prayers. There, all the married women in their gold and diamonds would sing prayers and exchange plates. All the little girls, like me, would look on in reverence and respect.

To my childhood eyes, the women resembled movie stars. How romantic it was that they prayed for their husbands in this way. Once the prayer was over, we would head home for the final ritual. First, my mother would observe the (almost always hidden) moon through a sieve and then touch my father's feet in respect. He would then feed her freshly squeezed orange juice to break her fast. Afterward, we would all sit down to dinner.

Ah, true love, I thought.

As I grew older, I began to notice the custom's prevalence in north Indian movies. I dreamed of the day I would be able to practice this with my husband. It seemed to be one of those things that would complete my transition to true womanhood.

I began planning weeks in advance. Since both my in-laws and parents lived in a different country, I knew there would be no one to help me decipher the customs here in the U.S. I was determined not to let that be an impediment to my perfect day, though. I researched as much as I could and called my mother many times to ensure that I had all the things that I needed.

The night before the big day, I prepared the *puri* dough. It was ready to be rolled out and fried the next morning. Ghee scented with cumin became my base for making the *aloo*.

Finally the morning arrived. I awoke at 4:00 a.m. Before my husband could say good morning, all four burners were going on the stove. Tea was simmering on one, *aloo* on the other, hot fried *puris* on another, and warm *kheer* (rice pudding) on the last one.

I sat down at four-thirty and ate my meal with great pride. I was sure I was entering some secret of womanhood that had long eluded me. My husband merely smiled as he drank his tea.

Off to work he went.

I had taken the day off work, as I had heard I was supposed to do. In the morning, I got my hair and nails done. The afternoon was spent meticulously applying henna to my hands and feet. As I waited for the henna to dry, I remembered the days my mother would do the same.

Around 5:00 p.m., I decided to get "properly" dressed. I had researched and found that on festive days women should wear *solah singar*, or sixteen adornments, on their body, and I now had all sixteen of them. I wore my wedding *lehnga* (gown) to mark the occasion.

Since we were new to the area, I did not know other Indian families nearby and so had decided to do the prayer at home. I began with reading Sanskrit scriptures.

Then the wait began for the moon. It hid until almost nine. Finally, I caught sight of it. I ran inside and got my prayer plate along with the sieve and orange juice. It was time. I looked at the wondrous moon through the sieve, dipped my hand in the glass of water on the plate, just as my mother had, and sprinkled the water at the moon. I closed my eyes in prayer and then bowed to my husband in a scene reminiscent of an Indian movie.

Then, as if to mark a milestone, I took a sip of the orange juice. Ah, I thought, this is what a true married woman feels like. I had done it. I had fasted on this very auspicious day to pray for my husband's long life. I was truly a devoted wife at age twenty-four.

Just then, as if on cue, the phone rang. My husband answered. As he talked, his expressions changed from a smile to giggles and then to laughter. "It's your mother," he said turning to me. "She wants to know if you are all set for the *Karva Chauth* fast tomorrow."

This story first appeared in the Christian Science Monitor.

Fasting for Love, Part 2

Growing up, this is the woman I wanted to be: newly married, draped in a red saree sparkling with gold and silver, heart full of love, stomach full of nothing. Once a year, married Hindu women from northern India observe a religious ritual called *Karva Chauth*. They fast all day, taking no food or even drink, and pray for the long life of their husbands. There are several stories of how the fast came to be, but they all led to one conclusion in my mind: women who fast for their husbands are more in love, more devoted, and can even defeat the god of death.

As a girl, I would follow my mother around on *Karva Chauth*, making mental notes, getting ready for when I would finally have the chance for my own love fast. Preparations started the night before: she would knead dough for fried bread and boil potatoes, seasoning them with cumin sizzled in oil, a ritual breakfast she had seen her mother and grandmother prepare for years. The morning of the fast, she would be up before sunrise and eat, sipping a cup of tea. Then I would watch my mother, hungry and thirsty, smile through the day's work. She would occasionally complain of headaches and lie down. She would feed us, but she would not touch the food. There would be calls all day from other fasting women; as they grew older, they used the time to talk about how bad the hunger pangs were getting.

Only after they see the moon can these women eat and drink again. I remember asking why, but no one knew. More than that: no one cared. It was the way it had always been. But there was a new twist in our family: my father would drive around, for hours sometimes, trying to find a perfect sighting of the moon so that my mother could eat again.

Dad would rush home and we'd all get in the car (after calling all the neighbors). He'd smile at my mother and tell her that he was so grateful to her and happy that she could break her fast soon. She would pray, look at the moon and then at him, and he would offer her the first sip of juice. And in his own personal tradition, he would always have a gift for her as a thank you. Mom would smile and open the box, her eyes twinkling, and Dad would hold her. Every year, seeing this, I knew my romantic ideal of marriage. (All the *Karva Chauth* scenes in Bollywood movies helped, too.)

When I got married at twenty-four, I could hardly wait for my first *Karva Chauth*. I was living in Washington, D.C., far from my mother, but it came and I did everything I had seen my mother do. I made fried bread and cumin potatoes, fasted all day and sacrificed for my husband. My heart felt good, but my stomach was in total disagreement. I was thirsty, I was hungry, I was cranky. I kept looking at the clock and warming up curses for the moon if it was going to hide that night. But when I finally broke my fast, I felt like I had achieved something only true lovers are capable of.

Then the phone rang. My mother called, to remind me to fast for *Karva Chauth* ... tomorrow. I cried: having prayed for his long life on the wrong day, would I cause my husband's early demise? I calmed myself down, eventually, but kept a special eye on my husband for months.

The following year, I rolled the bread, made the potatoes. I laid out my clothes for the night. But then a strange sense came to me of the old failure, and I suddenly felt unworthy—not good enough to defeat the god of death. I cried again. It's a simple thing to not eat for a day, but I was carrying with it the burden of tradition and the past, and I felt myself crumbling under my own expectations. I had failed at it once, and the magic that I had grown up under seemed broken. I didn't go through with the fast and ate solemnly.

After that year, on the day of *Karva Chauth* I could never shake that feeling. How could I even try? Would the fast even mean anything? I was young, an idealist—and an idealist doesn't easily accept failing. When my friends would ask me if I observed *Karva Chauth*, I'd dodge the question. I avoided calling my mother on the fast day. I skipped invitations to end-of-day prayers, ashamed.

But as the years went by, I noticed that my husband did not love me any less. "I don't understand how not eating for a day makes anyone a better anything, let alone a wife," he said one day as I lamented yet again at being unable to bring myself to fast.

It was then that I began to wonder about *Karva Chauth*. I asked friends why they fasted, and leaving aside insistent mothers-in-law and gifts at the end of the day, the answers boiled down to, "It's how it is; why change tradition?" For me, I realized that *Karva Chauth* was about wanting to feel that loving bond that I had seen between my parents. It was about belonging to that gorgeous group of Indian women who could do no wrong in their married life. It was about wanting to be the perfect wife. Could I only have those things brought to me by tradition?

One day, at the urging of my husband, I finally called my mother in India and confessed. The disappointment in her voice was piercing. "So, you are telling me that you eat on that day?" she asked quietly. She's called me every year since to remind me when the fast is.

But it was after that day that I decided to start a new tradition: each year, instead of a day of fasting and sacrifice, I turn the day of *Karva Chauth* into a day of nurturing. I begin preparations early in the morning as well, but instead of preparing for a fast, I prepare for a feast. I cook my husband's favorite dishes like lamb with green chiles and curry leaves, chile chicken with garlic and peanuts, rice layered with buttered sage and paneer.

"Mom, I am going to lay out the red plates so that everything looks like Christmas," my older child says. The house becomes festive, we fill vases with flowers, we dress in our best. But before we eat, we still wait for the moon to show itself. We drive around, as I have seen my father do for so many years, until we find it. I no longer shy away in shame from the *Karva Chauth* moon; instead, I smile confidently. I look up at it, with hands folded in prayer, and pray that my husband's dreams will always be touched with magic. After the moon sighting, my husband and I hold one another and my kids giggle at the scene. I am not sure they fully understand my tradition but I know this: they feel what I felt years ago when I saw my mother and father embrace under the *Karva Chauth* moon.

First published on Gilt Taste.

Green Cardamom

Green cardamom is a very popular spice in Indian cuisine. There are many reasons that I adore it, but I have to confess there is one special reason. Years ago when I first came to the U.S., I was a lonely graduate student trying to fit into this new world. It was hard. I remember making my mother's rice pudding to comfort myself. The cardamom I added to the pudding had an alluring aroma. Guess who it lured in? The man who would become my husband! It is true, I guess, the way to a man's heart is through his stomach!

The whole spice—the green cardamom—looks like a small pod and has tiny black seeds inside; both pod and seeds are edible. The flavor is lightly sweet. Some stores sell white cardamom, which is basically green cardamom that has been sun-bleached, but I don't recommend it. For best results, buy green cardamom in pods and use a mortar and pestle to grind it when you need it. I am often asked if I grind only the seeds or the whole pods. It really is your choice; I personally prefer the taste of both of them together. If you want to use only the seeds, open the pods, remove the seeds, and use as needed. Don't discard the pod—use it to flavor your morning cup of joe!

My favorite ways to use cardamom:

1. Add crushed or ground green cardamom to coffee or black tea.

2. Add a touch of freshly ground cardamom to hot chocolate.

3. Include cardamom seeds in any dinner roll or French brioche recipe.

4. Add some to your Sidebar or Moscow Mule cocktail for a remarkable new flavor.

5. Add to desserts like rice pudding or vanilla custard.

6. Try pairing cardamom with mint in your favorite mint cocktail.

7. Chew a whole pod (yes, the whole green pod) to freshen your breath—this is my MOST favorite use.

Food and Identity

Am I a Mango?

"What kind of food are you?"

What kind of an idiotic question is that?

I want to scream at the young reporter who asked me that question. I am in India for the summer, and I'm being interviewed for a magazine story. And his first question is: What kind of food are you?

At first his question annoyed me, and then it made me laugh. Perhaps I can just get away with being cheeky since this question could not possibly have a serious answer. "I am a mango," I say to him. Now can we move on? "Why?" he asks.

The look on my face tells him to move on and he does. After the interview, I begin to think, why did I say mango: luscious, ripe, delicious, and sweet-smelling? I am nothing like that. Not even close. I love mangoes. They are my favorite fruit, but I don't think I am like a mango at all.

I am actually thinking about this question. It is on my mind as I return to my father's Delhi home. I can smell cardamom wafting through the air. He is busy making me breakfast. We stand in his spacious kitchen in Delhi. It is wide and broad and full of steel utensils.

Dad is making *dalia*, a broken wheat porridge. He has made this for me for as long as I can remember. My kids are sitting at the breakfast table enjoying the porridge, which we have told them is the Indian oatmeal. They resisted at first, but then as soon as Dad added honey, they ate it up. He is making mine with cardamom, which I love.

"Will your American friends like this?" my father casually asks my twelve-year-old.

"What do you mean American friends? I am American, and I like it," is my son's instant response.

So easily, and so simply, my son could state who he is. Who am I, I wonder. My father prods my son, "So are you Indian or American?" There is no doubt in his mind: he is American. Dad looks at me. I am at a loss.

I was Indian. And now I don't know what I am. Why "was" Indian and not "am?" It is not because I don't love India now or don't want to be associated with the country of my birth. Well, I am the Indian of the India of the 1980s—the India of my childhood and the India of my youth. It was the India of barely kissed lips on Bollywood screens; it was the India of homemade pickles and mangoes dried in the sun for days; it was the India of joint families where aunties and uncles and cousins all lived together in small homes (and loved it); it was the India of running to the local vegetable vendor each night to get fresh vegetables for dinner; it was the India of scouring the footpaths for deals on clothes/jewelry; it was the India of one (BORING)

TV channel that showed a music program that we all eagerly awaited each week. I remember as a child, most people tended to stay in the same jobs for a lifetime. My father-in-law worked for the same company for thirty-five years, and this was typical. There were issues of poverty, dowry, women being discriminated against, and opportunities available only to those who had a fat bank account or a father with a fat bank account. For the common man, nothing was easy. I remember, years ago, writing an article for the *New York Times* about how the money coming in to the Indian economy was changing the way India eats. I thought that change was big. But now, it is bigger, far bigger than I could have ever imagined.

India today looks nothing like the India I remember and it begs the question: am I an Indian, today?

I visit only the larger metros when I travel to India, so I will preface the rest of this by saying that the metros are where I have seen the most change. I feel outdated as I wear my Indian outfits to Indian gatherings in India. The new, younger India seems more at home wearing Banana Republic or knockoffs of it. To be seen as hip, happening, and with-it, people dine at establishments that serve sushi, donuts, burritos. Indian food is keeping up and trying to modernize as fast as it can (*paan* Martini, anyone?). The pace of change is strong in families as women work outside the house. Women are holding amazing and powerful positions, something unheard of even until a couple of decades ago. There are hundreds of channels on TV, with hundreds of shows. Conveniences are the theme of the hour—you can call your vegetable vendor on his cell phone and he will deliver vegetables to your door, sometimes chopped up to your specifications; yogurt, bread, pickles, chips all are available in packages for your convenience. Oh, I love that! But it is all so new to me. I feel like an outsider in my own hometown, and I hate that feeling.

I was waiting at a mall for a cousin to show up when I noticed a customer arguing with a shopkeeper of a major brand-name store. I snuck up to listen. "How can you be out of all the clothes in my size—I don't understand!" the customer was yelling, and the patient shopkeeper was trying to explain to him that someone bought all the small sizes they had that morning. An average sweater there cost a few hundred dollars. Farmers are making money, as evidenced by the opening of Bose stores to sold-out crowds in Punjab, or the fact that people from surrounding areas in Delhi are hiring consultants to show them how to shop and match a Gucci bag with a Jimmy Choo shoe.

On my last trip to Delhi, my cousin informed me that now there was a Baskin-Robbins in India. But what I wanted was the ice cream of my childhood, Kwality's Vanilla. He looked quizzically at me as if I had stepped out of the Dark Ages. Eventually, we went and bought Kwality. The sweetness of the creamy white soft-serve reminded me of my summer vacation days in Old Delhi as cousins and I played under the brilliant sunshine. "We will make one stop," my cousin informed me and we stopped at the new ice cream joint. He convinced me to come in and I was stunned: saffron, mango, coconut, guava, *paan*—all the flavors of my childhood were now flavors of ice cream in India. I could not try the samples fast enough, and for the moment, the soft-serve Kwality ice cream was forgotten.

I remember going to restaurants in India and never ordering

anything to drink because I don't like beer and I don't drink scotch. Well, these past few trips, I spent more time ordering drinks than I did ordering food. Spiced cocktails blew my socks off. There were amazing wines from superb wine makers and lists of vodkas and rums that I have never seen even in the U.S. Even more than that, the crowd ordering the drinks is so smart about what they are having (a big change from five years ago when an Indian friend told me that I was a snob for not wanting to refrigerate red wine). Indians are traveling far and wide, and their interests and knowledge are something to envy. I don't know anything about wine, I admit openly, so at one restaurant I asked a random young couple to help me out. Not only did they order the wine for me, they asked me to join them for lunch. Both worked for big companies and traveled a lot. No kids, they laughed and said, "For that we have to be in the same room at the same time." She wore glittering jewels, which she saw me admiring. "You can get these at the costume jewelry place in south Delhi," she said, telling me where to buy them. There was a time, I remember, when wearing faux jewelry and not gold was a sign that you could not afford gold. And today, it is a fashion statement. I was thrilled because I am all about big, faux rings.

So where do I belong? Am I an old Indian, of the India past, or am I a new Indian of India today?

"Your breakfast is getting cold," my mother says as she puts the plate of wheat porridge in front of me. I can smell the cardamom, and I begin to eat.

The doorbell rings and it is the *dhobi*, the guy who irons our clothes, bringing back a lot of shirts he ironed. Then it rings again. This time, it is the errand boy from the chemist bringing the medication my father ordered. Within the span of a half-hour, the doorbell rings six times. This I do remember from my childhood, and it hasn't changed. The neighbor from next door stops by to deliver the wedding invitation for her son and brings along with it a large, fancily wrapped box of Indian sweets. And, finally, when I think the doorbell is going to drive me nuts, it is someone for me. It is the driver of a close friend of the family. "Aunty sent this for you," he says and hands me a steel box. I open it to find all my favorites: white homemade butter, a yogurt curry, and clove-scented basmati rice. Aunty has done this for the past ten years.

I go back to the table and eat my broken wheat breakfast.

I have found the answer to the question about my food identity.

The food that I am like is broken wheat. I take on the flavor of wherever I am planted. Growing up in the Middle East, I ate it with pomegranate molasses; when in India, I flavor it with cardamom; and when I make it for my family in the U.S., we now add maple syrup.

Enjoy Your Mango

A few years ago, I gave a speech on Indian food at the French Embassy in Washington, D.C., and I mentioned that I used garlic in my mustard-fish curry. An older lady approached me afterward, very upset. She had never heard of garlic being used in mustard-fish curry. How dare I spread myths about Indian food? I was really taken aback. My mother did it that way, I explained to her. My mother's mother did it that way, and we assumed my great-grandmother did it the same way. But no explanation would appease her.

Now, people often complain about the arrogance of the young, but still I had to wonder: how did she know that her recipe was authentic, and mine was not?

One of the most popular Indian dishes in Britain is chicken tikka masala, a dish of marinated, clay oven–roasted chicken simmered in tomato sauce. Estimates are that as many as 23,000,000 portions a year are sold in Indian restaurants in England alone. But there is absolutely no evidence that chicken tikka masala came from India. Its origins are in some dispute (England? Ireland? 1950s? '60s? '70s?). The most popular origin legend is that in the 1970s, a British chef poured Campbell's tomato soup over some leftover chicken tikka (marinated chicken pieces cooked in a tandoor), called it Chicken Tikka Masala—and the dish became a sensation. In 2001, Britain's foreign secretary called chicken tikka masala one of Britain's national dishes. Does that make it authentically British?

What does authentic really mean? Who decides what authentic is?

India is famous for its tomato-based curries, yet tomatoes were not even introduced into Indian cuisine until the 16th century—at the same time as potatoes. Chiles weren't used in Indian cuisine until sometime during the 15th century—amazing, considering authentic Indian food is said to be hot and spicy. Authenticity, it seems, evolves.

To avoid any further annoying exchanges on the subject, I decided to no longer use the phrase "authentic Indian" to describe a dish. I began to use "traditional." But inevitably I encounter self-proclaimed standard-bearers who run after some marker of "authenticity" (my mother made it that way, I tasted it this way, the superstar chef makes it this way) that may or may not have relevance to other people.

Years ago, when I first moved to the States, I hosted my first dinner party. My friends requested authentic Indian food and I tried my best to comply. We had cumin-scented potatoes, a shrimp-coconut curry, a vegetable pilaf, and several chutneys and pickles. Everyone loved the food, but then came the dessert: custard with fruits. "So, you didn't want to make an Indian dessert?" one friend remarked.

I was taken aback—how could a dish I had learned at the knee of my Indian grandmother and perfected under my Indian mother's watchful eye and eaten and served at almost all large family gatherings not be Indian? "I suppose," he went on, "this is a remnant of what the British may have left behind in the Raj."

Perhaps he was right that my grandmother or her mother had learned to prepare it during the British stay in India. But to me, custard with fresh fruits is as authentic and traditionally Indian as chicken curry. Authenticity and tradition are born out of the personal experience of the home cook and from the embrace of environment. Restaurants don't factor in because their menus are designed to cater to specific markets.

There is nothing wrong with learning about the history of a dish and its origins. The problem comes when that curiosity overrides common sense; when strict adherence to the "authentic" becomes rigid, judgmental, and a general pain in the rear; when having a dish denounced while you're enjoying it muddies the experience.

When I worry obsessively about something, my father reminds me of an old Indian saying: "*Aam khao, ped kyon ginte ho.*" Translated literally, it means: Enjoy your mango, and don't worry too much about which particular tree it comes from.

This story first appeared in Wine Enthusiast *magazine.*

The Chocolate Girl

I was seven years old and living on the tiny island of Bahrain. My father, an engineer, and my mother, a schoolteacher, had moved our family from India for a better life. A better life meant good things—like a brand-new, high-end stereo system. And I had decided to figure out how my father's brand-new stereo system worked.

As I sat on the floor of our living room with the completely disassembled, as in totally messed up, system around me, my father walked in. He was a gentle man but he was livid—I think it was the closest he ever came to spanking me. After he calmed down, he showed me how to fix the system. And then I quietly crept away to my room, ashamed and terrified of what I had done.

My father came in a little later to make amends, armed with a plastic container the size of a tiny take out box. It had a white spatula. On the cover of the container was a picture of a slice of bread smeared with chocolate and the word, "Nutella." I opened it, dipped the spatula into the tiny mound of creamy chocolate and then tasted it. The chocolate melted instantly on my tongue, its hazelnut flavor filling my mouth with new sensations. I gobbled the entire container in under three seconds.

One of my friends says, "You can only taste something for the first time once." That once was enough for me. And so began a love affair that has lasted thirty years and survived high school, college, broken relationships, marriage, dieting, moves, babies, layoffs, and career changes.

After that fateful introduction, all my meager pocket money went to Nutella. On my way to the school bus stop, I would stop and buy two containers from a talkative old Arab shopkeeper who had a store two blocks from our house. I devoured the first container immediately. As I sat on the narrow concrete steps that led to his store, his customers passed by and called me "*Fatat-ish-Shocola* (Chocolate Girl)." I carried the other tiny container with me to school, to dance class, to art class—everywhere. Eating the second packet was always dictated by how my day progressed. If I got teased on the bus for being too skinny, it was gone by the second bus stop. On good days, I would eat it on my walk home through the tree-filled streets. Nutella became a measure of my life's condition—it gave me great comfort during hard times and was a reliable friend on sunny days.

From Bahrain, I moved back to India, to Bangalore, to study for a degree in engineering and then to Virginia in the early 90s to get my master's degree. In the U.S., I discovered big things. Everything was big, and I could buy supersize jars of Nutella!

But this treasure came at a price: my Indian husband—whom I had met and married in Virginia—and my young son discovered it, too. Yes, I was selfish with it. Yes, I hid it so they would not finish it before me. Move over, Waldo. "Where is Mama's chocolate today?" was the game of choice in our house.

I took a career risk a few years ago and left a well-paying corporate job for a better-paying job with an Internet start-up. My timing was off. Instead of the Internet boom, I found myself in an Internet bust, and after a year I was let go. Having been raised in a culture where a job is for life, where you are defined by who writes your paycheck, I took it personally—really personally, as if I had been fired. My job was the reason we were in the States, away from home, and its loss hurt my confidence. In the same month, my husband, my sister, and my brother-in-law all lost their jobs. My world collapsed.

But my Nutella was always there, just waiting for me to take a loving dip into the jar. As my finger swirled in the chocolate, the taste took me back to childhood times with my father—back to my safe place. The taste promised me that everything was going to be fine—it proved great solace in a difficult time.

Even though I found another job, the loss helped me realize that I was not happy with my work and needed to do something else with my life. This realization and the death of a dear friend helped me make a life-changing decision to quit engineering and plunge head-first into writing—food writing, to be exact. I have always had a deep love and a great respect for food and culture and how they interact to affect our lives. I began to write about food. While some writers use caffeine or other lively libations, my constant writing companion has been my large jar of

Nutella.

Recently, after a seven-year struggle with infertility, I became pregnant again, and it was a high-risk affair. For three months, I was on total bed rest. That took its toll on my seven-year-old, Jai, who thought I had a bad back. I had not told him the truth because the chance of miscarriage was too high—it had happened twice already—and I did not want to break his heart again. "Why does your back always hurt, Mama? Why won't you play with me like you used to?" he asked each day.

One morning he got up early and I heard him brushing his teeth. Usually he would come to my room to see me after that, but on this day he did not. I figured he was upset with me for not being able to play.

Fifteen minutes later he showed up, clutching a hand-drawn get-well card, a jar of Nutella and two spoons. "Mama, on *Higglytown Heroes* they say that if you give someone a get-well card, they feel better immediately. This is for you. Now let's eat this for breakfast." I hesitated for a second—I was on a no-caffeine, no-junk diet—but after one look at his expectant face, I reached out to him. Somehow my father, living thousands of miles away, had appeared in my son's form. We ate the Nutella together—one big spoonful each.

Does Ethnicity Matter?

I thought it would only be appropriate to have a French meal as a precursor to a culinary trip to France. So I called a dear friend, a trained chef, to ask if he would prepare a meal for me that would open up my appetite for France. My kind friend obliged.

I sat in his warm and comfortable kitchen watching him passionately dole out dish after French dish.

We started with a sparkling consommé. As my friend poured some and garnished it with chervil, he explained the process of making it. "This consommé really is a rich broth. You know, the secret is to clear out the raft of egg white, mirepoix, and meat that forms on top of the simmering broth in such a way that we leave no particles behind. After straining, the broth must be crystal clear." It was—and so rich tasting I did not even think I needed another course!

Lobster thermidor, another French classic, was served in lobster shells. As my friend laid out the dish, I could see his eyes twinkle—you know, that twinkle when you know in your heart you've nailed a recipe. "All French cooking is really about learning to make the sauce. The more perfect your sauce, the better your dish will taste," he told me and went on to rhapsodize about the five French "mother" sauces and the secrets to making each of them. We kept eating as he showcased dish after dish.

It was some of the best food I ever ate. Decadence on top of French decadence.

And now, the moment of truth: My friend, Chef K. N. Vinod, is Indian, not French. Does this make his cooking any less French? Less authentic? Less amazing?

A few days after that dream dinner, I was in a taxi in Paris on my way to learn French cooking at a local school. My driver—a born and raised Parisian—was thrilled when I told him I write about food for a living (which I sometimes feel is like telling people I am a therapist, as they then feel compelled to share their opinions). "I hate to eat out in Paris now," he confided to me. "There are no French chefs cooking anymore. All the food is being cooked by immigrants, all these Indians, Turks and—" And he stopped, realizing perhaps I am Indian.

But his story reminded me of an incident at an Indian restaurant in Maryland. An Indian lady arrived at the restaurant—which boasts an open kitchen—saw Hispanics and other non-Indians cooking and left in a huff as the place was not "authentic."

I have been mulling over this question for a while now. Does the ethnicity of a chef matter? Do you have to be from Spain to cook a perfect Spanish paella? Do you have to be Indian to make the perfect curry? Do you have to be Irish to understand soda bread?

In this global world, it is hard to keep up, especially when it comes to food and cooking. There are more than 50,000 food blogs: I've lost count of how many cookbooks I get each week to review and how many cooking schools are popping up all over the world. We all want to learn to roll pasta like an Italian *nonna*, to make a tomato-coconut curry like a Goan, to perfect a béchamel sauce like a true French cook.

One of my favorite chefs in Washington, D.C. makes the most authentic Chinese food I have ever tasted. I've traveled around the world and always find myself comparing the Chinese food I eat to his—and his food wins hands down. But he is not Chinese, not by a long shot. Scott Drewno was born and raised in upstate New York. And he learned to cook Chinese food from … Austrian chef Wolfgang Puck.

"I love the multifaceted aspects of Asian food: there is so much texture, flavor,"Drewno tells me as I eat his perfectly cooked and spiced quail. "It is not flat and one-toned like some other classic cuisines. I love combining the salt, sweet, savory, and sour flavors to create dishes."

I get up the nerve to ask him if ethnicity matters.

He looks concerned, as do many chefs when I ask them this question. But he answers: "It is a complex issue. I think there are so many things that matter, but I do believe that a cuisine can be learned. My motto is one I got from Wolfgang: use good ingredients and don't screw them up."

Clearly, Drewno has broken the barriers of ethnicity: he is a Caucasian cooking great Chinese food. I am happy to learn that he is not the exception, but rather part of a growing trend. There is a Guatemalan chef making sushi in Washington,D.C., and according to reports, doing it very well.

Let us for a minute assume that the ethnicity of the chef is critical to making a dish. Do I then infer that all those books promising to teach me to make pasta like an Italian grandmother should be filed under "false advertising"? Or that the cooking school offering to teach me to cook like a native Parisienne is nothing more than a month of fun and frolic? Can authenticity in cuisine not be learned?

I grew up with the notion that good food is born of the hands of a good cook: someone who understands ingredients, understands that controlling the fire controls the food, and is immersed in the culture they are cooking from. My Indian friend can make authentic French food because he was trained by a French chef. He can also make authentic Indian food, not because he was born Indian, but because he learned that art as well. I believe an understanding of the culture whose cuisine you are trying to replicate is critical to the authenticity of any dish; being born in that culture is merely incidental. The culture teaches you the cuisine: you need Arborio rice to cook risotto (basmati will not do); cayenne and paprika are two different animals; "sauté" means something totally different to the French than to American home cooks.

In my heart I believe that recipes belong to the land: authentic ingredients can become miracles in the hands of a trained and passionate cook. The ethnicity of the ingredients, not the cook, is what matters.

A Day in Paris

Julia Child died on my birthday.

It was odd when I heard the news. I felt bad that my only connection to this legendary personality was death.

Of course, if I am honest, I should also admit that her persona intimidated me. Perhaps it was because I was intimidated by the cuisine that she talked so passionately about. French food to me was complex, complicated, difficult to learn, impossible to master, delightful in taste, and yet, like an unrequited love, something to be admired from afar.

I have recently become a child of new thinking about removing limitations that I place on myself and about testing my assumptions. After all, as they taught us in consulting school: ass-ump-tions make an ASS of U and ME.

So when I got invited to go to a cooking school in France, I jumped at the opportunity. And then I threw up a few times. What the hell was I thinking? How could I go to the *gastronomique* capital of the world without a clue as to what they do in the kitchen? And now, as a food writer, I would be expected to know at least something. I decided to cancel. Several times. But my husband kept reminding me of the "assumptions" I was making: I was no good; French cooking was hard; I was never going to be able to learn it; oh, and did I mention, I was no good?

I did not cancel, and I got myself on a plane to Paris. (Have we talked yet about the fact that I am terrified of flying? Well, chalk this trip up to pushing past our own limits. But let me discuss just one shortcoming at a time.)

Wide awake, adrenalin pumping after a seven-hour-long flight, I arrived in sunny, bright Paris. I met the rest of the team[1] who would be there with me: Tim, a young, flamboyant writer from New York; Mina, a talented travel writer; and Jasmine, a beautiful, former sports star turned writer. My first thought was, well, at least the rest of the group looked sweet and not formidable. Of course, even though they appeared half my age (I later learned that baby-faced Jasmine was touching forty), they were a well-traveled lot, having recently been around the globe from Dubai to Jerusalem.

Cook'n With Class is a cooking school located in the heart of the cultural district of Montmartre. I had Googled the area before getting there. The reviews of Montmartre were mixed, tending more toward "stay away from it, it is a tourist trap." I wondered how the place would be. And I learned another lesson: don't read reviews. Nothing could have been further from the truth.

---

[1] Names have been changed for privacy.

The area, while bustling with tourists and locals, is a snapshot of a city drenched in culture and, of course, a love of food. The area is dotted with darling little cafés. Other types of restaurants—Indian, falafel, kebabs—are sprinkled on every street. Vendors line the streets, showcasing everything from pink-skinned chicken breasts to white salmon to rabbit to the most luscious strawberries from Spain. The old buildings in the area are not just a testament to times gone by, but their walls hold secrets yet unknown. A plain, boring white shutter on the third floor of an old building boasts a wild array of sunflowers. "That window belongs to the flat where Van Gogh lived and painted when he was here," a passerby tells me. As I walk around, I am struck by the names on the walls—Picasso lived in this house, and there is a bust of the singer Dalida near a children's playground. The bust says it is one of eight. "The original was stolen, this is the first fake. The others are round the city," is the explanation. The weather—it is early spring—is crisp, clear, with skies so blue you wonder if there will ever be clouds again. Assumption number one is shattered: that it always rains in Paris in springtime.

I stood outside the school, unsure if I wanted to enter. The entrance was inviting: a quiet door with a small sign. At least it didn't look intimidating. Chef Eric Fraudeau, who owns the school, was nothing like the stern, tall Frenchman wearing a sparkling white chef coat who was ready to pounce on my every ignorance, as I had imagined. Instead, I met Eric: a jolly, funny man who made me feel right at home. "I was hoping to learn about spices from you and see how we can incorporate that into our class," he said. Learn from me? My assumptions were indeed making an ass of me.

Eric built the school, he told me, to share his love of cooking with everyone in his hometown. The classes the school offers range from making simple to fancy desserts, baking, spending a day at the market, and learning about cheese and wine. And what is more, and unusual for Paris: the classes are offered in English. Eric spent many years in the United States heading Michelin-starred kitchens and then returned to his home country to build a life for himself and his bride Yetunide. His demeanor was casual, nothing like what I was expecting. My whole theory that the French were stern, did not like foreigners, and did not like to speak English was being quickly demolished. Of course, we justify our thoughts to ourselves all the time! I thought, this is fine—he is nice but wait till the cooking starts. Then the attitude will show. And I will be right.

My fear of French cooking had started, strangely enough, when I became a food writer. All of a sudden, I went from being a simple home cook to being viewed as an expert cook: two very different things. I loved to cook, I loved to share my world, but by no stretch of the imagination was I a chef capable of creating dream-like gourmet delights. I began to stick with cuisines that incorporated spices: I understood how sizzled cumin could affect a potato or how a paste of garlic and ginger could provide a base for a curry. But I found myself distancing my mind from cuisines that were not rich in—or that I thought were not rich in—spices. French stood out. I did not know the sauces; I did not understand how to marry cream with butter; my fear of baking stood in the way of understanding breads and pastries.

As the day dawned for the first class, I stood in the shower of my small, rented Parisian flat, shaking. A little terrified, a little worried, and very ashamed. Today was going to be the moment of truth: they would know that this food writer did not understand their food or the techniques they used. I was disheartened, angry with myself for not reading more, for not leafing through all of Julia Child's books, for not being like Julie Powell who cooked her way through difficult French dishes (well, and easy ones, too).

But the show had to go on, and I showed up at the farmers' market where the class was going to start. Our teacher, a gorgeous woman with bright eyes and a pixie haircut, was Chef Constance. I smiled. She reminded me of Chef Colette in the animated movie *Ratatouille*: she was spunky, full of energy, and had a no-nonsense spirit around her. The group began to introduce themselves, and when she came to me, she asked, "And what is your name?"

A simple question. I know my name. It is Monica. But as I stood there in the glittering Paris sun, soaking in the noise of the crowds, the strong smell of the coffee, the energy of the city, I thought, well, at this time, what if I wasn't Monica—the Monica filled with fears and intimidated to be here? What if I was, what if I was Monique?

"I am … Monique … I like that name better than Monica," I said to her. The group began to laugh, "Oh, you do look like Monique, and that is what we are going to call you." Chef Constance took to calling me Monique, along with the rest of the group. Funny how a little, stupid, silly joke can change your whole point of view.

From that point on, I became Monique. The group, all

youngsters, got something to giggle about, and I got something else to set my mind on instead of my ignorance.

Our first stop, after the market, was an inviting Parisian cheese shop. All I knew about cheeses was that I liked creamy and hated stinky. Our guide, luckily, knew a lot more. Constance is from the heart of France, but her father, she told me, grew up in the north where "they eat smelly cheese and drink lots of beer." She walked around explaining different types of cheeses; the art of making the cheese; the importance of the region the cheese comes from; the rinds, the colors, the smells. The strange array of white and yellow slabs shelved around the store, which moments ago had seemed alien and difficult to comprehend, now became objects of wonder and respect. It isn't that I had never read or written stories about cheese, but when someone explains something to you with such passion and vigor, the ingredient takes on a whole new meaning. "See, look at this cheese! Do you know why it is hard and not soft like the other cheeses? It comes from the mountains and so it has to travel well. And see this butter, it is made from fresh, raw milk. One taste of it, and it will change your life." And I instantly knew that she was probably right. What struck me most was that her talk focused on tradition and the importance of preserving culture. What I had heard of the arrogance of the French was actually totally wrong. It wasn't arrogance at all: it was pride in a rich and deeply rooted culture.

It reminded me of the spice markets I had visited in Delhi a year earlier, as I had walked around Khari Baoli—Asia's largest wholesale spice market—with a culinary historian. Every stall had a history: the pepper came from the villages of the south;

the salt came from the mountains; the mustard came from the fields of the east. Each person selling the spices had a story: their family had been there for years; the store had traditions of how they sold what they sold ... My mind wandered into the similarities and differences. While the French had upheld their ingredients, we Indians had not shown the same respect, I felt, toward our spices. But things were getting better back home.

"Monique, Monique, are we ready to leave?" Chef Constance taps me on the shoulder. I am not used to my new name yet. I smile sheepishly and follow her out. As we leave, I notice the owner of the store is scrubbing the ground outside the store with a small brush. She is vigorous and diligent. Pride, what an amazing sentiment.

Our next stop is a butcher, and as we reach it, I realize we have lost half our group. One writer is afraid of birds, so going into the butcher shop was a no-no for him. Another writer is a vegetarian, so there was no chance she was going in, either. I smile, as their absence makes me feel like it was okay to be different and not know—or like—everything.

Ah, the Parisian butcher shop: not a place for the faint of heart. As Chef Constance explains the ratings on the butchered chicken, rabbit (with the heads) and other meats on display, my friend and writer extraordinaire, Kathleen Flinn, pokes me in the shoulder. "Do you know why rabbits are sold with their heads on?" she asks. "So you know they are not selling you cats." I guess you never know!

"We don't change butchers here; a butcher is like your family doctor. You go to the same one each time." While the voice mouthing those lines was from Chef Constance, my mind is hearing them coming from my father. He says the exact same thing! I begin to feel my body relax as I realize that, perhaps, I am not as ignorant about the food here as I think I am. But it is early in the day, and so far we are only picking out familiar ingredients.

We keep moving, and now the group was all together again. We buy peppers and cauliflower and onions. As we pick and smell and touch the vegetables for freshness, I realize that I sniff just like Chef Constance—only she looks way cuter and more sophisticated when she does it, and I look like a dork!

Our last stop before we head into the kitchen is the seafood stall. A tiny shop with big fish! Chef shows me how to select the fish: the eyes, the scales, the firmness of the flesh. We pick squid, and she tells me she will show me how to clean it. We also pick a gorgeous rose-pink salmon.

Armed and ready to cook, we arrive at the cooking school. Everyone is laughing and giggling, and I begin to feel my nerves starting to act up again. What if I make a fool of myself?

I stop myself: Monique is not scared. She is ready to learn. She is a learner, and she is smart and talented. She can do this.

And we begin. Sleeves get rolled up; knives come out; the chopping begins. Chef Constance is focused, giving directions, passing ingredients, moving the group toward the goal of making a meal.

I watch her carefully: the way her eyes focus on the bell pepper as she begins to chop it; the way her neck arches when she reaches to look down at the caramel boiling; the strength in her hands as she teaches me the right way to hold a pan and *sauté* apples so that they jump and then land in the pan just so. We begin to discuss our passion for cooking. "I learned to bake when I was eight," she tells me. "Others were taking ballet classes and I was making pastries." But you know, I could tell, that passion comes from within.

"Yesterday I bought these shears that have multiple blades ... They are said to be great for cutting herbs," I tell her proudly.

"Those are for moms! Let me show you how a professional does it!" she says. And I see it again: pride in perfect technique and no easy way out.

And then, I see something that catches me by surprise: Chef Constance eyeballs a lot of ingredients but doesn't measure anything she uses. I did not think that was allowed in French cooking! I grew up in the bosom of *andaza* cooking—estimation cooking—where a little of this and a little of that are the way to go. I see her doing the same: she eyeballs the salt, the pepper, the olive oil. She focuses on the pan to listen to the sizzle of the salmon and presses it down with the spatula. Experience, I can see, has taught her the right time to flip the fish so that it is perfectly cooked. The precision that I had heard the French were so famous for comes the next day when we learn to prepare macaroons. But then, I have to remind myself, precision in baking is true in any culture, not just French. And no matter how hard I try, I would never be baking macaroons at home. It is just never going to be my thing.

As we prepare the dishes, I find myself confident—and that catches me by surprise. The group goads me on with many shouts of "Go, Monique!" as I attempt to poach an egg enclosed in plastic wrap, sauté apples in a pan, or pipe cake batter into a mold.

Chef Constance keeps reminding us that the key to making good food is to use fresh seasonal ingredients and try not to monkey around with them too much. Like the apples: we found aromatic, ripe apples. Just a light sauté in butter, and they were ready to go. The salmon: picture-perfect pink; just seasoned with olive oil, salt, and pepper; kissed by the fire; and ready to serve.

I keep chopping, keep watching her, keep learning: the cauliflower all needs to be cut to the same size (she sounds like my mom); carefully pick the bones from the salmon (she sounds like me); pay attention, this is important, this is a really good technique for … (she sounds like every passionate chef I have ever learned from).

Our menu includes a foamy soup made from purple carrots seasoned with cumin; a creamy cauliflower velouté garnished with parsley; seasoned poached eggs atop red peppers and softly cooked onions, garnished with fried walnut bread; pan-seared salmon and chili-spiced calamari with a side of roasted cauliflower; a selection of cheeses; and cake for dessert topped with sautéed apples and drizzled with caramel cream sauce.

So what was that deep fear that had been nagging at my spirit?

It was, in retrospect, a fear based on ignorance and limits I set on my own views. Total ignorance.

What I learned was how similar my world and the world of French food really are: a passionate focus on great ingredients. Yes, there were dishes that were very complicated, but the same is true in any cuisine. There are so many techniques and dishes in Indian cuisine that I have not yet mastered, but I am not afraid of it due to—I guess—familiarity. After spending two days at the cooking school, I realized that I would never be a master of French food, either. And you know what? That was okay. The bigger win was that I was no longer afraid.

"I love to travel," Chef Constance tells me when she learns of my love of spices. "I like going to Thailand when I have time to learn about the spices there. I want to make a cuisine by using my family roots, my French culture, and a mix of the things I see."

I smile at her. And I love to learn about other cuisines, take them back with me, and apply a little of what else I know to them to create something that is uniquely my own: life on a plate.

When I returned home, I posted on Facebook: Dear Julia Child: I now totally understand your love and affection for the culture and food of Paris.

After all these years, I finally have a meaningful connection to Julia Child.

Prayer in a Cup

My cooking has saved me from myself many times. I have cooked through miscarriages, through broken friendships, through painful breakups, and through deaths.

But not any more and certainly not today.

The pain sears through my abdomen.

I bend over the stove. One hand steadies my wobbling body. The other hand, automatically, goes to the site of the pain. As though touching it will somehow make it stop.

The pan on the stove is hot; the spices are sizzling. I am sorry they are going to burn. I cannot move. My world begins to go dark. I clutch at the site of the pain. Hoping, anxiously, that it is the last time. It will never be. I know. I hope it is a mild attack. I have never had a mild attack.

The pain rises. This time, I am sure, it will be the one that pushes me over the edge. The nausea is competing with the pain, as if trying to outdo it.

"How bad is the pain now?" my doctor had asked me on my

last visit.

How bad? Like a knife cutting though my flesh, like labor pain—only there is no baby at the end—like being crushed by a big truck.

I just look at him and say, quietly, "It hurts a lot."

He is a patient man, and I know he is frustrated. My pain frustrates him because he cannot solve the problem. There is severe scarring inside my body. Scars and adhesions cause the pain. There is no way to take them away; there is no way they will heal. This pain is part of my life. His job is to heal. He cannot heal. He can only help me manage this pain. And sometimes not well. The medication has been changed so many times that there is not much left to do.

I smell the spices burning. The pungent aroma fills the air. I want to move but I can't. The spasm hasn't passed. It is meaner than last time. Stronger than last time. Or, perhaps, I am just weaker.

The first year the pain started, six years ago, I was sure it would pass. I mean, how much could scar tissue really hurt?

I found out the hard way. Some things in life are just hard.

I begin to straighten myself. The spices are a mess. I throw the mixture into the trash, cursing.

I am not yet stronger than my pain.

I look around for the medication. I find it. After much debate and much discussion, I am on meds that are said to be non-addicting and non–habit forming. The funny part: they make my face itch like crazy. I hate that even more than I hate the pain. But it isn't as debilitating as the pain.

I have learned over the years to be grateful for the pain. The pain is just that: pain. It is not part of an illness that is getting worse. There is power in being grateful, at least I am told. The endless tests reveal that there is nothing else causing the pain. In its defense: it is steady, consistent, disciplined, and recurring.

The worst part about being in pain is the lack of appetite. All the allures of my kitchen hold no attraction. There could be a curry simmering on the stove; a golden, luscious cake on the counter; a glittering piece of chocolate at my beck and call. My beloved food takes a back seat. My family has learned to help: they hand me my hot water bottle, give me hugs and kisses and my meds, and then stare helplessly.

I am not always in pain. It happens a few times a year. But it really does show up at the least opportune times: my son's first piano recital, my TV debut, a restful night. And it lingers. The medication takes a few hours to kick in. In those few hours, I feel the sweat, the bile, the blood curdling. I struggle to sit, to lie down, to stand.

Why so much pain in this world? I ask my father repeatedly.

"Perhaps God wants us to pray," he says. His answer is always the same.

Yes, prayer. But when it hurts so, even prayer is hard. I curse a lot, which I guess does not help!

After reading several books on pain management and learning my own pattern, I settled on the only thing that helps me: being in my kitchen.

Now, instead of just praying for the pain to recede, I always go to my kitchen when the pain starts. I learned the hard way that I could not actually cook through the pain: I was in the kitchen during one particularly bad episode and bent over and held a steaming pot during the spasm. It was only after the spasm passed that I realized I had burnt my fingers.

Instead of cooking, I pour myself a cup of steaming hot green tea with a few basil leaves. I know that I will never drink it.

I stand in my kitchen, sometimes holding the cup, sometimes just leaving it on the counter. I always bend to smell the basil and the sweet gentleness of the tea. Tea has always had dear memories for me ... sitting with my parents and sipping warm chai, listening to my grandmother slurping her tea from a tea saucer, hanging out with aunts over a cup of ginger tea and biscuits. A cup of comfort ... always reminding me that things can and do get better, and that just like all good things, all bad things pass, too. I try to breathe in the scent of the tea. The scent and the memories hold me for the seconds (or eternity) that it takes for the spasm to pass. As long as the tea is hot, I will be in pain. The engineer in me has figured out that if I time the medication right, it kicks in just as the tea starts to get cold to the touch.

I breathe it again, this time with a prayer. And again.

I move away from the stove and toward the sink.

I clinch my fists and scream silently as the spasm passes. I know from experience that I have a few minutes before the next one arrives.

The cooking, right now, will have to wait.

I reach up to the cupboard and grab a teabag.

This story first appeared in Spirituality & Health *magazine.*

Saffron

I cannot think of another spice that has inspired so many songs, so many poems, so many books, so many dreams, and so many people! Saffron, said to be worth its weight in gold, is not only a spice good for adding aroma and flavor, but is still considered to add a touch of luxury to a dish. As a child, I recall my grandmother adding saffron to dishes when we were expecting guests. It was her way of honoring them. Saffron is used all over the world—and not just in food. In Tibetan Buddhism, water perfumed with saffron is one of seven traditional offerings to the Buddha.

Saffron also has been found to have medicinal benefits. It has been shown to be more effective than Prozac for helping cure symptoms of depression. A friend of mine who sells saffron for a living once told me, "If you eat too much saffron, you will die laughing." It wouldn't be a bad way to go.

My favorite ways to use saffron:

1. Use sparingly, since its flavor is strong. As a general rule, about three strands per person in a recipe should be enough.
2. Saffron is water-soluble; the best way to use it is to soak it in warm water, in warm milk, or, as they do in Persian cooking, in rose water for a few minutes to allow the spice to release its color and fragrance.
3. Add to clear soups for a lovely flavor and color.

4. Pair with fish curries and fish stews.
5. Add to your herbal tea for an added dimension.

Food and Faith

An Ode to Whole Roasted Chicken

If you are looking for a recipe for whole roasted chicken, you won't find it here. I am not sure there is one, since each time I make this chicken, it is a little different. But it always has one element that is the same: it is comforting. I never grew up on whole roasted chicken. My mother would always buy cut-up chicken, marinate it, and roast it that way. It tasted amazing.

It was here in the States many years ago that I first saw someone roasting a whole chicken, and it fascinated me. The possibilities seemed so endless—how to marinate it, what to stuff in it, and what vegetables to roast with it. This became my fun meal of choice; each time I tried something different. First, it took me the longest time to learn how to roast the chicken until it was cooked. I don't have a poultry thermometer, so I would keep taking the chicken out every 20 minutes to see if it had cooked. My lesson learned was that the crispiness of the skin is NOT an indicator of how well the chicken is cooked. After many, many disasters, I learned that the chicken was done when

I cut through the leg joint and did not see blood, and the liquid ran clear. I usually now roast my 3 1/2-pounder at 400 degrees for about an hour and thirty minutes. That gives me the doneness I like and does not overcook the chicken.

Then I learned about the skin and how to crisp it up. I tried so many different marinades like yogurt, lemon juice, olive oil—and oh, so much more. I learned that nothing crisps up the skin like butter. Plain and simple. Butter rubbed all over the bird will really help the skin crisp up. Oh, one more thing: I never used to pat the bird dry before doing all that I was doing to it, and it never cooked just right. Now I take the time to pat it really dry and then add my butter and seasonings.

Speaking of seasonings, this is where I love to play. I have tried harissa, sriracha, Indian tandoori masala, fenugreek leaves (that version made it into my cookbook, *Modern Spice*) and so much more. Happily, most results are great and really worth trying.

And as for vegetables, I have found that any roots or hard vegetables work well. I usually make a bed of sweet potatoes, onions, squash, or whatever else I have. Season it with salt and pepper and a bit of extra virgin olive oil, and then put the chicken on top.

To truss or not to truss? I never trussed since most of my chickens are so small! But if I do truss, then I do a simple tie— nothing fancy.

Into the oven, and then the waiting begins. Once the chicken is cooked, I pull it out and let it rest, covered, for about 20 minutes. The juices that collect in the pan all go into a saucepan. I just heat them up and let them thicken, and then serve them on the side. I don't think this is the authentic way. I think you are supposed to add flour and butter. I don't. The juices along with the taste of the vegetables just seem to shine through without my messing a lot with it. So why try?

I haven't learned to carve like Martha yet. I make a mess each time. I watch the videos, have friends show me—but that is an art that still eludes me. The best part of that? I get to make more chickens till I learn how to get it right.

There is something so elegant about a whole roasted chicken. Perhaps it reminds me of all the holiday commercials I used to watch on TV in the U.S. when I first moved here. I was lonely, and my only outlet was the TV and reading magazines and books. Many a time I would encounter a gorgeous photo or video of a whole roast chicken and marvel at the warmth it seemed to generate at the table. Something about it says there is enough for everyone and more. Something about it whispers "I care."

Perhaps I am too sentimental.

It has been a rough few months around the world. I have had friends lose dear ones and family members fall seriously ill. In all this time, I find myself turning to my husband and kids for comfort and all of us, in turn, turning to food.

Food has such power, wouldn't you agree? Not only to nourish but to give us comfort in difficult times. Each time I step into the kitchen these days, I am grateful for all that we have received and all that we can share.

The smell of a chicken roasting in the oven always assures me that all is well in the world.

Star Anise

Star anise is so aromatic that sometimes I feel it is unfair to the other spices I use along with it! Yes, it overpowers most everything. But then again, perhaps that is its reason to be! I love its licorice-like aroma and sweet taste, which is very similar to anise (but the two aren't related). If you have never seen it, it is a pretty spice—dark brown and in the shape of a star, hence the name. Oh, yes, it is also on the cover of this book! It is most closely associated with Chinese, Vietnamese, and Japanese cuisines; in fact, it is one of the key ingredients of the famous Chinese five-spice powder. While it is also associated with Indian food, I never tasted it growing up and actually first encountered it only a few years ago, when I was trying to learn to cook Malaysian food. If you enjoy your spirits, you may be familiar with the taste, as star anise is a key ingredient in sambuca, pastis, and Pernod.

Whole star anise is actually dried slices of the star anise fruit, with anywhere from five to 10 points to the star. They can be used whole or ground. Just remember to use the spice sparingly—it is very strong. If you use whole or broken pieces, discard them when done.

My favorite ways to use star anise:

1. Infuse it in simple syrup, and then use that syrup to flavor drinks and desserts.
2. Use it in your favorite curry recipe.

3. Pair it with cinnamon and use to braise your favorite meat.
4. Pair it with cinnamon, cloves, and bay leaves to flavor the cooking oil before cooking simple white rice. It will add terrific aroma to the rice dish.
5. Use it to flavor jams and compotes.

Food and Writing

Does a Recipe Need To Be Complicated To Be Good?

I was so proud of my cookbook, *Modern Spice*. That is, until the moment a reader approached me at a fundraiser. "Your recipes are too simplistic," she blurted out. It threw me for a loop—too simplistic? I developed *Modern Spice* keeping contemporary people's busy schedules in mind. My focus was to create and share recipes that did not sacrifice taste but delivered on the "ease of preparation" promise.

The reader who approached me said that she had prepared my pan-seared trout with mint-cilantro chutney, but feared it wasn't really cooking because it was so simple. At first, I felt I had failed her. I wondered if I should apologize. Had I been unworthy of my readers' trust? Had I let them down?

I probed her a little, and her response surprised me even more. She loved the dish, and so did everyone who ate it. But it did not fulfill her cooking aspirations. "Indian cooking is supposed to be hard," she said. "And this book made it seem easy. That isn't real Indian cooking, right?"

Wait—isn't being able to cook something that's pleasing the point of a good cookbook? Does a recipe need to be complicated to be good?

I think what isn't necessarily obvious to many who read and cook from cookbooks is that creating simple recipes is often more difficult than creating complex ones. Conjuring a recipe that relies on only a few ingredients, yet sends your taste buds into an orgasmic frenzy, takes a great deal of understanding of ingredients: how they work individually, how to make them work together in perfect harmony, and how to cook them just right. It takes years of experience to learn, and to be able to teach, "simplicity." And that is my goal as a cooking teacher and a cookbook author—to teach students to be able to cook on their own.

It takes a lot of experience to prepare "simple" just right. In simple recipes with just a few ingredients, there's no place to hide. It takes guts—and culinary prowess—to cook that way. Please be aware that when I refer to simplicity in recipes, I don't mean dumbing down recipes. Yes, there are plenty of people who promise that our lives will be easier if we follow their "simple" plan to combine the contents of five tin cans for a meal. To me, that's a false economy of time and money, not to mention flavor.

My parents taught me how to cook—how to smell a melon, peel an onion, sear a fish, sizzle cumin. But most important, it was from them that I learned why freshness in ingredients matters so much and how a perfectly ripe tomato needs nothing more than a sharp knife to bring out its best. I grew up without a can opener in the house. My parents bought all their ingredients fresh. The only time I remember there being canned anything on the table was when my father fell in love with British baked beans and brought home several cans each time he traveled to London.

Instead, I grew up with spices and herbs. Our recipes would be considered incomplete without them—and yet I never remember my mother using ten different spices in a dish. A few in the right combination always did the trick. I once received an e-mail from a reader who was really angry that one of my recipes for tea included only one spice. "Are you afraid of spices?" he demanded. On the contrary: If you know how much flavor a single good-quality spice—say, cardamom—can add, why would you add flavors that muck it up?

So what exactly constitutes a simple recipe? To me, it is a recipe that requires just a few ingredients, is smart in the way it uses those ingredients, doesn't require my entire paycheck, and teaches me something. *New York Times* food reporter Kim Severson wrote a piece some time ago on "deal breakers" in recipes, in which she decried a particular recipe for requiring fresh pig's blood and another for demanding fleur de sel from buckets of seawater. Not happening in my kitchen.

Ask someone what their favorite dish is to make at home and rarely will they announce "foie gras with bacon air, mint puree and pine nut confit." Most times you will hear squash soup, light-as-air buttermilk pancakes, mom's recipe for lasagna. Yes, there is great joy in going to a restaurant and enjoying a complicated meal cooked by a legend like Daniel Boulud. But cooking at that level at home each and every day is neither possible nor desirable for most of us. I have kids, and as the

Boston *Globe* so kindly put it, my recipes are "clearly the work of a mother cooking on weeknights." Even so, I bet Chef Boulud would agree with me that good recipes come from learning how to use ingredients wisely.

A chef who masters this art of simplicity isJosé Andrés. I recently prepared a recipe of his for slender stalks of asparagus bound together with thinly sliced Spanish ham and pan-fried. That was it: Asparagus. Ham. Pan-fry. Why is this notable? Those of you who know José will know. Those of you who aren't familiar with him, let me tell you: José Andrés is a disciple of Ferran Adriá, a chef who regularly thrills at culinary innovation, who can deconstruct a glass of wine on a plate and who can wrap a drop of olive oil in sugar. But he is also a husband and a father who clearly understands his role as a home cook as well as his role as a cookbook author and teacher. He demonstrates this with an ability to show readers what they can make at home without a nitrogen tank handy.

Should José's great-tasting asparagus recipe have made me feel like I wasn't cooking?

Cooking teacher and great TV chef Sanjeev Kapoor, who has sold millions of books, once told me that true culinary genius lies in knowing how to teach people to master dishes they can easily create at home. It does not, he continued, lie in showing off what the chef knows. The scale of complexity in recipes is in no way a litmus test of how good or bad a recipe is.

This story appeared in Best Food Writing 2009, *edited by Holly Hughes.*

Turmeric

I love turmeric. Here's why you should care about this lovely golden powder: the *American Journal of Epidemiology* reported that a diet high in curry (which typically includes turmeric) may help the aging brain. As reported by Reuters, "Curry is used widely by people in India and 'interestingly,' the prevalence of Alzheimer's disease among India's elderly ranks is fourfold less than that seen in the United States." Think about it—fourfold!

What exactly is turmeric? It is a rhizome (underground stem) that looks a lot like the fresh ginger you can buy in markets. It is most popular in its ground form—that gorgeous yellow powder. When using the powder, a little goes a long way. A little adds a toasty flavor; a lot adds bitterness. How much is ideal? I usually add 1/2 teaspoon to a dish that serves four.

My favorite ways to use this spice:

1. Add 1/4 teaspoon of turmeric, with a pinch of black pepper and toasted, ground cumin seeds, to olive oil and lemon juice for a quick salad dressing.
2. Toss with roasted vegetables.
3. Add to rice, quinoa, oats, and porridge dishes.
4. Add to meat dishes, soups, and stews.
5. Add to any curry dish containing coconut milk.

Acknowledgments

"Don't tell her anything. She will use it in her next story," a friend of mine once remarked. This book is living proof that he is right! I am very grateful to be surrounded by family and friends who not only support what I do but warn others about the perils of hanging out with me!

Thank you to my husband and my kids and everyone in my family.

My amazing supportive FB team and beta readers who are all part of a group called Monica's Muses.

A huge shout-out goes to Mike Klozar for helping, guiding, mentoring me as we created the proposal for my upcoming food memoir. He is truly an amazing editor and friend. Kathleen Flinn deserves a special thanks and possibly a huge award for standing by me through thick and thin.

The superb cover for this book was designed by James at Humblenations.com. Thanks to Jason Anderson for all the great formatting. And, of course, A HUGE thank you to Simi Jois for her amazing pictures.

A big thanks to the editors - Suzanne Fass, Bridget Testa, and Elizabeth Young who fixed all my crazy typos and then some.

About Simi Jois

Simi Jois, a marketing and branding professional, found her true calling in culinary photography. Simi has always been intrigued by light. Rays of sunlight streaming into a forest or the gentle embrace of light on a bowl sitting on a dark table capture her eye.

Growing up in a home that emphasized art, Simi's mind was subconsciously trained to engage creatively with color, texture, light, shadow, and composition. She uses photographic images as her canvas and the lens as her brush. She did not have to look far for a subject—her passion for creating flavors provided her with infinite permutations of expression. Painting with ingredients, pairing exotic spices for mutual enhancement and richness of flavor, Simi narrates her stories through the play of light and bold strokes of color.

Simi believes that her love for creating unique flavors deeply informs her passion for culinary optics. Her work has been featured on MSN (Food & Drink), *Fox News* magazine, *Better*

Homes and Gardens, and The Kitchn. She is a frequent contributor to The Daily Meal.

Simi enjoys reading and has a deep affinity for esoteric texts such as the Scriptures. She loves to study Renaissance painters. She likes to travel and has traveled across the U.S. and Europe.

Simi's portfolio : http://www.simijois.com
Simi's blog : http://www.turmericnspice.com

About Monica Bhide

Monica Bhide is a culinary cultivator, explorer, and teacher—as well as her family's resident chef. When it comes to food, she's just as curious about the how and the why dishes are made as she is about the influences that different cultures have in today's kitchen.

A storyteller at heart, Monica combines her love of family, friends, and food—along with personal anecdotes highlighted by her Indian heritage—to help people add an exotic, unexpected, and most-welcome new element into their lives.

She's the author of three cookbooks: *The Spice is Right: Easy Indian Cooking for Today*; *The Everything India Cookbook*; and *Modern Spice* (Simon & Schuster, 2009). *Modern Spice* was also customized for the Indian market and published in India by Random House.

Additionally, she has been published in national and international publications, including the *New York Times*; *Food & Wine*; *Cooking Light*; *Bon Appétit*; *Saveur*; *Parents*; *Prevention*;

Health; *SELF*; and in several *Best Food Writing* anthologies. She frequently contributed to NPR's *Kitchen Window*.

Monica was the recipient of the Susan B. Langhorne Scholarship for Food Writers at the Symposium for Professional Food Writers in 2004 and was the runner up for the 2005 and 2010 awards. She won a full Greenbrier Scholarship in 2011.

The *Chicago Tribune* named Monica one of the seven food writers to watch in 2012. In April 2012, Mashable.com picked her as one of the top ten food writers on Twitter. Her work has garnered numerous accolades, including the inclusion of her food essays in *Best Food Writing* anthologies (2005, 2009, 2010, 2014).

Monica truly embraces the spice of life. Her mantra is to eat locally but cook globally. Enjoy tradition, but search out change. Respect technique while adding a playful twist. And enjoy every opportunity to connect with family and friends through good food.

She lives with her husband and two sons in northern Virginia.

Visit her website, monicabhide.com, for recipes, stories, and more!